ADVENTURES IN
GRAPHICA

ADVENTURES IN
GRAPHICA

USING COMICS AND GRAPHIC NOVELS TO TEACH COMPREHENSION, 2–6

TERRY THOMPSON

Stenhouse Publishers
Portland, Maine

STENHOUSE PUBLISHERS
www.stenhouse.com

CREDITS

Pages 44 and 96: *The Battle of Gettysburg: Spilled Blood on Sacred Ground* by Dan Abnett. Illustrated by Dheeraj Verma. Copyright © 2007 Rosen Book Works. Used with permission.

Page 44: *The Battle of Shiloh: Surprise Attack!* by Larry Hama. Illustrated by Scott Moore. Copyright © 2007 Rosen Book Works. Used with permission.

Page 45: From *Hot Iron: The Adventures of a Civil War Powder Boy* by Michael Burgen. Illustrations by Pedro Rodriguez. Copyright © 2007 Stone Arch Books. Used with permission.

Pages 53 and 73: *Marvel Age Spider-Man #8* © 2008 Marvel Characters, Inc. Used with permission.

Page 56: From *Babymouse: Queen of the World*, copyright © 2005 by Jennifer Holm and Matthew Holm. Used by permission of Random House Children's Books, a division of Random House, Inc.

Page 62: From *Marvel Age Spider-Man Team Up #1* © 2008 Marvel Characters, Inc. Used with permission.

Page 66: From *Tiger Moth: The Fortune Cookies of Weevil* by Aaron Reynolds. Illustrations by Eric Lervol. Copyright © 2007 Stone Arch Books. Used with permission.

Page 69: From *Harriet Tubman: The Life of an African-American Abolitionist* by Rob Shone and Anita Ganeri. Copyright © 2005 David West Books. Used with permission.

Page 83: "Owly and Wormy: Aw Nuts!" by Andy Runton. © 2004 Andy Runton. Used with permission.

Page 87: From *Robin Hood* by Aaron Shepard and Anne L. Watson. Illustrations by Jennifer Tanner. Copyright © 2007 Stone Arch Books. Used with permission.

Page 93: From *Marvel Age Fantastic Four #7* © 2008 Marvel Characters, Inc. Used with permission.

Page 98: From *The Adventures of Tom Sawyer* by Mark Twain, retold by M.C. Hall. Illustrations by Daniel Strickland. Copyright © 2007 Stone Arch Books. Used with permission.

Page 99: From *The Day Mom Finally Snapped* by Bob Temple. Illustrations by Steve Harpster. Copyright © 2007 Stone Arch Books. Used with permission.

Page 107: From *The Bermuda Triangle: The Disappearance of Flight 19* by Jack DeMolay. © 2007 the Rosen Publishing Group, Inc. Used with permission.

Page 112: From *Chinese Myths: The Four Dragons* by Tom Daning. Copyright © 2007 the Rosen Publishing Group. Used with permission.

Page 114: From *Babymouse: Heartbreaker* by Jennifer Holm and Matthew Holm, copyright © 2006 by Jennifer Holm and Matthew Holm. Used by permission of Random House Children's Books, a division of Random House, Inc.

**LIBRARY OF CONGRESS
CATALOGING-IN-PUBLICATION DATA**

Thompson, Terry, 1970–
    Adventures in graphica : using comics and graphic novels to teach comprehension, 2-6 / Terry Thompson.
        p. cm.
    Includes bibliographical references and index.
    ISBN 978-1-57110-712-1 (alk. paper)
1. Comic books, strips, etc. in education. 2. Reading comprehension—Study and teaching (Elementary) I. Title.

LB1044.9.C59T48 2008
372.41'2—dc22

2007051350

Cover and interior design by Isaac Tobin
Cover illustration by Lauren Nassef
Typeset by Isaac Tobin

*Manufactured in the United States of America
on acid-free, recycled paper*

14 13 12 11 10 09 08   9 8 7 6 5 4 3 2 1

> *True heroism is remarkably sober, very undramatic. It is not the urge to surpass all others at whatever cost, but the urge to serve others at whatever cost.*

ARTHUR ASHE

This book is dedicated to all the teachers who've purposely made it their lives' work to teach in higher-needs schools and lower-income areas—those genuine superheroes, with whom I'm fortunate to work on a daily basis.

CONTENTS

ACKNOWLEDGMENTS

On Sunday evening, May 23, 1999, for the first time in her life, seventy-two-year-old Broadway actress Elaine Stritch took the stage to accept a Tony award. Not two minutes into her acceptance speech, millions of fans across the country watched in disbelief as the orchestra interrupted Ms. Stritch too early, and she was ushered off the stage. I feel a bit like that now. I may never write another book. I may never get another chance to express my appreciation to all the folks who've supported me on this journey and who've helped make this book a reality. I want to thank so many people, but I know I have to be brief.

First and foremost, a special thanks to Russell Qualls, whose smile, laughter, energy, and support lend a sense of perfection and serenity to every new day, and whose belief that I could take over the world if I'd just focus my energy on one project is only equaled by his complete respect and total understanding that I wouldn't be the person I am if I weren't constantly spinning plates. You're my favorite!

To my parents: my mother, Marie Flory, who gave me the belief that I could reach my dreams, and my father, Jim Thompson, who gave me the drive and the work ethic to make it happen. To Dwight Flory, Tonie Thompson, Eloise Cass, and Jimmy Cass, my pseudo parents, who came into my life much later, but whose pride in who I am and whose encouragement in every endeavor I make are just as sincere and authentic as a real parent's.

To Angela Ford, my dearest friend, who shares the same brain with me, who bequeathed to me the secret knowledge of the strength behind invisible Wonder

Woman bracelets, and who is the only person in my life who recognizes that the one-word phone call—"Mexican"—means that: 1) an emergency has occurred, 2) this is not a drill, and 3) chips and queso will be required.

To the "T-Gang," Kimmy Parker, Stormy Gorman, Becca Heiner, and Jen Sultenfus, whose friendships know no limits and who always seem up for a spontaneous stress-reducing activity—whether that means I decide we'll all be learning how to make tamales, I bring a road trip to a screeching halt in order to take a picture with Scooby's Mystery Van, or I compel the entire gang to dress up like Willie Nelson for the rodeo.

To Dwight Price and Brandon Sampson, whose friendship, humor, and endless supplies of grilled cheese and cottage fries when I couldn't afford my own will always be remembered. To Yuri Ellett, who makes me feel like I'm a far better teacher than I ever could be.

To Joni McEvoy, Humble ISD Reading Language Arts Director, whose insights, feedback, and friendship kept me on target, and to my dear friend and fellow literacy coach Jane Flanagan, whose response to this project was perfect.

To Ken McLeod—supervisor, mentor, believer, and friend—whose conversations kept me going during the rough patches and whose rare music collection kept me company while writing in the wee small hours of the morning.

To Ellen Sankowski, the first person to clue me in to the fact that other people might be interested in hearing what I had to say on this subject, and to Marsha Garelick, a new friend, whose gracious manner and expertise in publishing encouraged me to move forward with this project.

To Philippa Stratton, Stenhouse editorial director, whose uncanny ability to continually giggle throughout my retentive meltdowns has been both comforting and disconcerting at the same time, and whose gentle, guiding hand gave me room to work but kept me reined in. To Erin Trainer, editorial manager at Stenhouse, whose assistance in tracking down copyright permissions was invaluable. To Jay Kilburn, for his tireless efforts in making this manuscript perfect.

To fellow Stenhouse authors Jen Allen, Franki Sibberson, David Booth, Max Brand, Tony Stead, and Debbie Diller, whose kind words, feedback, thoughts, and assistance helped me keep this project on track.

To the various publishers, authors, and creative teams who've so graciously allowed me to reproduce clips of their work in this book, and to graphica guru Robin Brenner for sharing her top ten list.

To all the teachers who welcomed me into their classrooms to work alongside them during this project, and who helped me chase down permission slips for photographs and work samples— specifically, Stacey Landrith, Mindy Butler, Daphne Trumbull, Elaine Hallford, Andrienne McKay, Sue Ladwig, Angela Riegle, Lindsay Lee, and Tomi Christman.

To Dorriene Reeves and her fourth-grade writing workshop, who were with me through much of this process and whose almost collective, in-unison response to this manuscript's acceptance—"We're going to be published!"—reminded me that I would not be writing this book alone.

To the principals of Humble ISD whom I've been privileged to work under while pursuing this project: Karen Geffert, who encouraged me to stay "green and growing"; Karen Weeks, who respected my work and supported the development of this book without hesitation; and finally, to Betsy Cross, who believed in my vision for our neediest students.

To the Humble ISD literacy coaches, reading recovery teachers, media specialists, and instructional technologists, as well as the staff, parents, and students at Jack Fields Elementary and River Pines Elementary—all of whom have offered assistance or support in one way or another. With that in mind, a special thanks goes out to the River Pines Elementary Frog Moms. Go Frogs!

To the Conroe ISD literacy cadres (the "literacy prophets"), for their enthusiastic interest in my work, their reception of my ideas, and the comforting hospitality of being among "my kind of people"—specifically, Melinda Donnellan, Laurie Koen, and Amalia Bruce.

To River Pines Elementary literacy coach, Carla Johnson, a new partner in crime whose instant friendship, rapport, support, and excitement for this project arrived on the scene just in time.

To whoever invented Tivo, Hot Pockets, and Pibb Zero, without which I probably would have starved and gone insane while writing this book.

And finally, to Terry LeJeune—the kid next door in Chapter 1—who was the first person to share his comic books with me.

Cue the music . . .

CHAPTER ONE

YOU GOT COMICS?

"Bradley."

"Bradley, I need you to focus."

"Huh? Oh, yeah. Right, Mr. Thompson."

Feeling my frustration mounting and steeling myself for yet another exhaustive tutoring session with Bradley, I mustered up my calmest, most encouraging teacher voice and repeated, "What were you thinking when you slowed down at that last hard part?"

He was tired. I was tired. The entire universe was tired.

We've all had one. You know you have. That one student you just can't seem to reach. You keep slugging away, sometimes seemingly beyond hope—and despite the temptation to give up, you remind yourself that this is why you're in this profession. This is what you were meant to do. So, you do what countless educators have done before you. You carry on. You keep at it. You plug away.

Bradley and I weren't strangers. In fact, we'd spent a lot of time together. One might say we were old pals. Now in fourth grade, Bradley had been on my radar since first grade, and, despite my most heroic efforts and some great classroom teachers along the way, I'd never seen him motivated to read.

Yes, we've all had one—and Bradley was mine.

As I regained my determination, I redirected Bradley's attention once again. But something felt off. Bradley's inattentiveness seemed different than usual; he wasn't drifting off to his regular dream world. He was intent. And focused. And staring at the cabinet behind my desk.

Resisting the urge to roll my eyes, and once again calling on the serenity of my inner teacher, I asked, "Bradley, what are you looking at? What's got you so distracted today?"

Without looking away from the cabinet, Bradley simply pointed his chin toward the lower shelf and asked, "Is that a comic book?"

• • •

In hindsight, I truly had no idea what I would do with that comic book. I've always been a visual person, and even though I wasn't a comic book reader as a child, I was routinely drawn to them. My family couldn't afford extras like comics when I was younger, but a kid in my neighborhood had tons of them. I loved those rare rainy days when we couldn't play outside—those were the days we got to go over to his house and dig through his comics. Even now, as an adult, I can't resist the lure of a comic book store. Somehow, just being among comics makes me feel like a kid again.

So it's no wonder that, as an adult, I've made a habit of ducking into comic book stores, and this visit was no different than the others. I went to the mall that weekend to purchase a birthday gift and ended up in the comic book store, looking around. That's it. Just looking. I never actually bought them. I just loved digging through them. Besides, the idea of taking up comics as an adult made me feel a bit odd. Admittedly, I was uneasy. Here was a medium I'd longed to understand since childhood, but discomfort kept me from really diving into it.

Then I saw it: one single shelf of comic books set aside for elementary readers. The teacher in me took over. I thumbed excitedly through several of the options and—hastily choosing an issue—made my way to the counter, paid for it, and ducked out of the store.

I wasn't really sure what I had, but somehow I felt its potential. I remembered how much I wanted to read comics as a youngster and thought that maybe, just maybe, I could find a way to use them in an instructional way. Pleased with my purchase, I pored over it while I grabbed a quick bite to eat at the food court.

I was enthralled, but unsure of exactly how I would use my delightful discovery. I vowed that, when I had some extra time, I would give it another look from an instructional viewpoint. But you know how it is. Upon returning to work the following Monday, duty and my hectic schedule called—so I put my little comic book on the shelf in my office, where it sat for three weeks, collecting dust.

Until Bradley found it.

• • •

"You mean that? That up on the shelf?"

"Yeah!"

"Yes, that's a comic book. I didn't know you read comic books, Bradley." What I *knew*, in fact, was that Bradley didn't read much of anything.

"Well . . . I don't . . . I mean, I want to . . . I . . . well . . . can I read that one?"

Now, in my entire history of working with Bradley, I'd never once seen him ask to read something. It wasn't for lack of trying on my part. Here was one of those moments where everything just clicks—a teachable moment, if you will, and I'm never one to pass up a teachable moment. I immediately scrapped the plans for the day's lesson and got the comic book down for him.

A side of Bradley I had never seen before emerged. He actively read and discussed the text, the pictures, and the story line. He was excited! I was excited! And the universe? Well, I like to think the universe was excited for us, too. We had so much fun reading together that I almost didn't notice that Bradley was ten minutes late for lunch.

"Wow, Bradley, our time's up. I've kept you too long again, and you're late for lunch."

Then something downright fantastic happened: Bradley asked if he could take the comic book to lunch with him. I was beside myself! "Of course you can take it to lunch with you! Just promise to bring it back tomorrow, so we can talk some more about it." We said our good-byes as I ushered him toward the cafeteria and then floated to the lounge to heat up my Hot Pocket thinking all the while to myself: Yeah, there's something to this . . . now I just have to figure out what it is.

But before I could figure it out, something even more amazing was about to happen.

Before I continue, you should know that I'm a literacy coach for a K-5 Title 1 school in a suburb of Houston, Texas. (At the time, I was also the campus testing coordinator for our state reading test.) Needless to say, if you're a struggling reader and you're on my campus, you'll eventually get to know me—usually sooner than later.

It seems Bradley showed his class the comic book during lunch, and it caused quite a stir. By the end of the day, three of my struggling fourth-grade readers had somehow risked certain fury from their teachers by ditching their classes to make their way down to my office.

Each one without a scheduled lesson.

Each one covert and clandestine.

Each one asking, "You got comics?"

WELCOME TO THE WORLD OF GRAPHICA

So, it all started with a struggling reader and a comic book, and I've been hooked ever since. Seeing the potential of this medium firsthand drove me to pursue an action research plan of my own: I absorbed any piece of information I could find about using comics in the classroom.

It wasn't easy. The Internet is littered with useful resources, but the search itself can be confusing and overwhelming—not to mention time consuming. Most of the books in my professional library barely mentioned comics, if they mentioned them at all, and I had difficulty finding appropriate comics to use in the classroom. When I did hit a gold mine of resources for the medium, the lessons and information often were geared toward high school or middle school learners, and I had to really tweak them or move on to another resource. Along the way, I found some useful resources and some not-so-useful ones. I had to feel my way much of the time and get creative, but I was driven.

Eventually, I settled on a fairly decent pile of ideas, pointers, and resources. Part of the information I've collected is a product of my own meager creativity combined with my working knowledge of best practices in literacy. Part of it is a culmination of my search for resources on using graphica with elementary students. Part of it is just good old trial and error. In the past few years, I've hit the road and become known as "that comic-book guy," as I've shared my insights in workshops, presentations, and classrooms. Along the way, I've discovered teacher after teacher just itching to get their hands on this information.

My intent in writing this book is threefold. Initially, I want to give you some background information on the world of comics by offering some theory, research, and support for using them. Then I want to share with you some opportunities to apply graphica to what we already know is good teaching. Finally, I want to offer some resources to use when you leave this book and continue your own learning. Throughout the book, I will share my own journey through personal anecdotes, research, and connections to the topics at hand. Along the way, I'll offer hints and suggestions that I've found helpful. Ultimately, I hope to leave you with a better understanding of the considerable power to teach and motivate students that can be found in this wonderful and exciting medium.

SHORING UP SEMANTICS

I've noticed that a lot of people seem confused when I mention that I use comics in my teaching. It isn't unusual for teachers, peers, and friends to bombard me with quizzical faces and comments like, "Are they comics? Graphic novels? Cartoons? I'm confused!" One workshop participant even stopped me, mid-sentence, during one of my presentations to ask for clarification by demanding, "What exactly are you talking about here?"

You may be feeling this way, too. You might think that you can never be completely sure you're 'saying it right'—and you wouldn't be alone. For instance, many comics diehards wouldn't hesitate to criticize my use of the term *graphica* (even my computer's insufferable spell-checker won't recognize it!). And, just as there are folks who would think we are talking about comedians when we refer to *comics*, there are just as many out there who would think we are referring to something far more sinister when we use the term *graphic*.

What's worse, most sources I've turned to only seem to add to the confusion. Depending on who or what I consulted in my research, their definitions may or may not have matched up. Even when I did find some similarities in terminology, certain nuances remained unclear. I was, however, relieved to learn that it wasn't just me who was confused.

You might find this hard to believe, but many researchers and professionals don't seem to agree completely on how best to define this medium. Offerings range from the vague to the extremely detailed, as we see from the following contributions:

- Sequential art in book form (Gorman 2003, xii)
- Tell a story with words and drawings and have an identifiable beginning, middle, and end (Cary 2004, 10)
- Stories told in both pictorial and word form (Foster 2004, 30)
- Arrangement of pictures or images and words to narrate a story or dramatize an idea (Eisner 1985, 5)
- Juxtaposed pictorial and other images in deliberate sequence

THE EVIL COMIC BOOK

If, at this point, you're concerned about the lingering feeling that comics are bad for kids, you wouldn't be alone—but have no fear! Though this common misconception has strong roots in the history of American culture, it has long since been debunked. For more information about how comics acquired such a negative connotation, and how research and time have led to its deconstruction, see Appendix A, "The History of Graphica," and Chapter 3, "A Word About the Research."

THERE'S A FIRST TIME FOR EVERYTHING

If you've never had a personal reading experience with graphica, and you are looking for a great place to start, I suggest that you pick up a copy of Art Spiegelman's Pulitzer Prize-winning graphic novel, *Maus: A Survivor's Tale*. In this engaging memoir, Spiegelman retells his father's experiences surviving the Holocaust. The author peppers the graphic novel with vignettes of interactions between him and his father, giving the reader an extra layer of story line that offers connections to themes such as family struggles, generation gaps, and adult children dealing with aging parents who are products of their past.

intended to convey information and/or to produce an aesthetic response in the viewer (McCloud 1993, 8)

So then, how do we describe a medium that seems so difficult to nail down? Perhaps a true definition for graphica is such a slippery beast because it is an ever-evolving medium with a wide range of possibilities. Scott McCloud, author of *Understanding Comics: The Invisible Art*, argues (after taking about twenty pages to define the medium!) that "our attempts to define comics are an on-going process which won't end anytime soon" (1993, 23). In addition, the authors of *Graphic Novels in Your Media Center: A Definitive Guide* mentions that "no one has ever developed a word that encompasses the rich and unique nature of comics all at once"(Lyga and Lyga 2004, 15).

I believe we can incorporate aspects from all of the various descriptions out there to create a working definition that suits our purposes. This would give us a common vocabulary and ensure that we are all on the same page. You'll notice that, within the descriptions just mentioned, the intent is essentially the same. So, without further adieu (drumroll, please . . .), I present to you my definition of graphica assembled by merging comments from the available research and scholarly writings:

> Graphica   *noun*   A medium of literature that integrates pictures and words and arranges them cumulatively to tell a story or convey information; often presented in comic strip, periodical, or book form; also known as comics.

Whew! That's certainly a mouthful, but I think it will do for now. If you dissect it, you'll observe that I included a few extras. Specifically, I added the idea of graphica being literature and also highlighted its cumulative nature and its integration of pictures and words. There's a method to my madness here. Up until this point, these aspects generally have been ignored. However, I think that these three additions are vital to the very purpose of this book. As you continue to explore graphica, you will begin to see that it does, indeed, have literary merit. In subsequent chapters, we'll discuss how the pictures and the words in graphica merge to produce a unique reading experience. Additionally, we'll explore how the cumulative nature of the medium correlates with comprehension strategies. Finally, you'll notice that I included the idea that graphica is also known as comics—in this book, I will use the terms interchangeably.

DIFFERENTIATING BETWEEN MEDIUM AND GENRE

Now that we have a working definition of the medium, let's turn our attention to the different ways it can manifest itself.

In order to do this, we need to review the *medium-format-genre* hierarchy. Essentially, the *medium* we are talking about is graphica, but it uses many different *formats*. Additionally, these formats are available in many different *genres* (ALSC Research and Development Committee 2006, 49; Brenner 2006).

In my early inexperience, as I first started working with graphica, I took to calling it a genre. As my awareness grew, I corrected this misinterpretation. I came to understand that graphica is actually a medium in which a multitude of genres are available. This can be confusing, so it might be helpful to imagine this idea using the analogy of television. The medium is television, but the formats—such as news, sitcoms, movies, commercials, public service announcements, and so forth—vary greatly. The genres covered in these formats can be anything from nonfiction to horror to biography to realistic fiction and more.

Comics work in much the same way (see Figure 1.1). You may think I'm playing with semantics here, but I've come to understand that, whether we're contemplating graphica or any other resource, it is especially important for us to make this distinction clear in our classroom discussions of genre. For example, many students and adults assume that graphica is only available in fiction. In truth, it comes in just as many different genres as other media our students read, like picture books, magazines, and chapter books. If we were to believe this assumption, we would miss out on everything that graphica can add to the regular genre studies we do throughout the school year. In addition to all the other wonderful ways comics can be used instructionally, they can offer great visual examples of the various genres students will encounter in traditional texts.

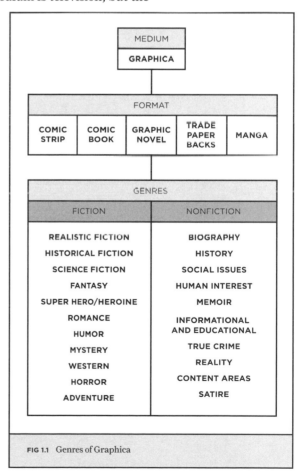

FIG 1.1 Genres of Graphica

FOCUSING ON FORMATS

Now, let's take a closer look at the various formats in which the medium of graphica is available. The more common formats are comic books, graphic novels, trade paperbacks, manga, and comic strips (see Figure 1.2).

FIGURE 1.2
Characteristics of Different Formats of Graphica

Medium	Format	Characteristic	Example
Graphica or Comics	Comic Strip	• Three to eight panels • Newspaper "funnies" • Recent rise in availability online	*Peanuts*
Graphica or Comics	Comic Book	• Periodical issues • Thin—durability similar to magazines • Story generally continues from issue to issue	*Spider-Man*
Graphica or Comics	Graphic Novel	• Book length • Sturdier durability • Story line starts and ends within same text • Can be anthology of previously printed comic books	*Maus*
Graphica or Comics	Trade Paperback	• Anthology of previously printed comic books or story lines	*Spider-Man Team Up*
Graphica or Comics	Manga	• Japanese-style graphic novels • Stylized drawings • Simplified features and outlines • Some read from back to front	*Dragon Ball Z*

COMIC STRIPS

Most of us are quite familiar with comic strips. You probably see them in your daily newspaper, but they can appear just about anywhere—including, more recently, online. They generally include three to eight frames that follow a quick, short story line.

COMIC BOOKS

Most people are familiar with comic books even if they've never read one. These little gems are multiple-page paperback offerings that generally are issued monthly. They tend to carry the story line over from one month to the next—often in a cliffhanger format. Comic books are widely known for their representation of popular superheroes, but you would be wise to avoid limiting them to just that. Today's comic books focus on a wide range of story lines that might surprise you.

GRAPHIC NOVELS

Graphic novels follow a format similar to that of comic books but differ in that they tend to have full-length story lines, meaning that the story starts and ends within the same book. Thicker than most comic books, graphic novels are bound like a book and are sometimes offered in hardback. Like comic books, graphic novels cover a wide range of topics and themes in addition to the more familiar superhero story lines. These topics can range from surviving the Holocaust concentration camps to the events of 9/11.

TRADE PAPERBACKS

Trade paperbacks (also known as TPB) appear in a similar format to graphic novels but are essentially anthologies of previously printed, usually popular comic-book issues. It isn't unusual for a comic-book publisher to offer an entire series of a top-selling comic book's story arc in a collective, bound format (Foster 2004; Lavin 1998).

MANGA

Because it is published more for middle school, high school, and young adult readers, *manga* is a form of graphic storytelling that I'm just now becoming more familiar with. We are starting to see more manga published for the elementary-aged student, specifically from companies such as Papercutz and Tokyopop (see Appendix E, "Publishers Offering Graphica," for more information). Similar to graphic novels in format, manga tends to use the more stylized Japanese illustrations to represent characters in a surprisingly distinctive way. Additionally, manga is often written for specific genders, separating works into *shojo* for girls and *shonen* for males (Fallis 2005; Brenner 2006). A quick search online will give you hundreds of examples of manga's format and style. The next time you're in one of the larger bookstore chains, you might ask to see its manga collection, as well. Many stores now have entire sections dedicated to this specific style of graphic storytelling. A word of caution with manga: at times, its story lines can be more mature than other comics. In addition, if the issue you are reading is directly translated from its original Japanese format, the story may read from the back of the book to the front, and the text from right to left (Fallis 2005). Keep these issues in mind if you shop for manga for your own classroom.

CARTOONS

At this point, you may be wondering about cartoons. When I discuss cartoons, I'm referring to the single-box format: an illustration accompanied by correlating text underneath. Sometimes, cartoons have speech bubbles embedded in the artwork. Often, these illustrations take humorous forms, but their purpose can vary (for example, satirical political cartoons). You probably have one in your email inbox right now. I've chosen not to include the cartoon format in our discussion of graphica for two reasons: 1) many scholars would argue against it being included (McCloud 1993, 20; Lyga 2004, 17); and 2) because the delivery takes place in one panel, cartoons don't really fit with the cumulative nature of the medium mentioned in our definition.

WEBCOMICS

One final note on graphica formats: I have specifically chosen not to include webcomics, a format of graphica available online, in this discussion. That's not to say that they wouldn't be included under other circumstances. Webcomics, in my opinion, are a valid addition to the various formats under the graphica heading. However, because the Internet is such a fluid medium, and because webcomics are a vast and constantly changing area, I have chosen not to focus our attention on them in this book.

HOW DO I KNOW IF THIS IS GOOD FOR MY STUDENTS?

You already do. You know your students as readers. You know their interests, their complexities, their worries. You know those kids who are fantastical and those who are more grounded in reality. You know which little ones need a new medium to explore, and which ones need something a little tantalizing to boost their interest in reading. In upcoming chapters, I'll discuss specifically how comics can be appropriate for children and how they can be used to support literacy instruction in your classroom, but for now let's think about the needs of your individual students. Many of them will find comics valuable, but some won't care a lick for them.

When Hurricane Rita hit southeast Texas in the fall of 2005, all the members of my extended family were temporarily displaced, and my twin brother's family came to Houston to stay at my house. We enjoyed our visit, but his kids began to get bored without any of their belongings to keep them busy. My niece Megan, just entering second grade, was knee-deep in a Junie B. Jones phase, so I brought home some extra books from work to share with her. For my nephew Tyler, a capricious fourth grader, I brought home some of the comic books that were popular with my own fourth-grade students.

Tyler's a smart kid with an incredible imagination, and I was excited to share my comics with him. So you can imagine my disappointment when, after skimming the front and back of a few copies and flipping through the pages, he simply muttered "Huh," tossed them on the counter, and went outside to play. In the end, he was more interested in my PlayStation than anything else.

I learned a valuable lesson that day. Just because I like graphica doesn't mean my nephew—or every kid I work with, for that matter—will like it too. Even though I introduce each different format with vigor, kids ultimately choose titles for independent reading based on their own interests and background. In essence, yes, comics are good for your students—but allow for mixed results. For some, comics will be nothing more than a passing interest, while for others, they will be the best thing to happen in their young reading lives. When all's said and done, your students' reactions to comics will tell you whether they're good for them. Go with it.

FINDING A PLACE FOR COMICS IN THE LITERACY BLOCK

With little effort, graphica can be integrated easily into much of what you already do. Research shows that students who read high-interest, self-selected texts for longer periods of time become stronger readers. Thus, simply allowing comics as a choice for individual reading time in the reader's workshop can be an easy incorporation. Students will snatch them up, and all you have to do is offer a few mini-lessons on the medium and add titles to your classroom library as you come across them.

Because comic books are relatively inexpensive (most cost about three dol-

FINDING APPROPRIATE TITLES

When teachers are new to the world of graphica, they often ask me about finding titles and making selections that are appropriate for the classroom. You can locate answers to these questions and concerns in Chapter 10, "Making the Right Choices," as well as in the appendixes, where you'll find useful websites, book titles, and even a list of publishers.

FIG 1.3 In Angela Riegle's second-grade classroom, weekly comic strips are cut out, placed in bins, and made available for independent reading during reader's workshop.

lars), collecting enough copies of a title to use with a guided reading or strategy focus group can be an inexpensive endeavor. But don't limit yourself to just comic books; tons of graphica can be found in the daily paper. Do you have colleagues who can't start their day without coffee and the newspaper? Make a deal with those early risers in your building to collect their comics section each day, and you've got limitless, multiple copies of comic strips to use in your lessons. Have your students clip copies of your class's favorite titles, and collect them in individual binders or bins for independent or paired reading time (see Figure 1.3).

I encourage you to double-check this, but it is my understanding that you can make an overhead copy of portions of certain texts and use it during your shared reading time without violating copyright laws. There are restrictions and guidelines, of course, and copyright fair use can be quite confusing, so you'll want to do your homework in this area. See Carol Simpson's book *Copyright for Schools: A Practical Guide* or the website *www.techlearning.com* for more direction in navigating the various copyright and fair use issues to ensure that you are within the intent of the law.

Finally, if you haven't done so in a while, check out some of your favorite publishers. Many makers of your favorite read-aloud and guided reading titles, having recognized the power behind graphica, are beginning to offer new and unique titles of their own. See Appendix E, "Publishers Offering Graphica," for more details.

BEFORE WE CONTINUE

By now, you might have noticed that I'm a driven teacher. I want the best for my students, like most of us do. The same holds true for the teachers I coach: I want learning to be fun and engaging. I'm reflective in my work, and I strive to produce students and teachers who are reflective thinkers as well.

Personally, I avoid cookie-cutter reading programs or the "sheep mentality" that often sweeps over our profession. I hold my calling sacred and choose not to leave the direction of my teaching to some nameless entity. I don't trust my responsibility to just anyone. I admit that it can be difficult, but I believe in differentiating instruction to meet the needs of my learners. In all of this, I find that graphica can sometimes fit the bill.

Yes, that's right: sometimes. Not always, and not in every situation. Graphica is a wonderful medium with a great deal of untapped potential, but I don't use it above all else. I use what works to get the job done, and sometimes that's graphica. I use graphica in a supplemental and integrated way—just like I would with any other resource.

So, as you move forward through this text, be aware that I'm offering you only a slice of what I use in the classroom. This book is an attempt to give you a fine-tuned view of what is, for most teachers, an unfamiliar and challenging medium, and I invite you to use it as a resource as you move to integrate graphica into your literacy block.

CHAPTER TWO

THE LURE OF GRAPHICA

FORBIDDEN PLEASURE

Turns out that Bradley's friends, the three struggling fourth graders from Chapter 1, were not alone in their assumption that access to the world of graphica could be gained only via stealth missions.

Not long after I let Bradley borrow my comic book, I checked in with one of my struggling third-grade readers. He had recently transferred to the school from another state and wasn't adjusting to life on our campus very well. I finally found him splashing water on another student in the first-grade hallway and called him over to me. After a short conversation about the school's expectations with regard to water throwing and a similar exchange with him in an attempt to find out what he was doing on the complete other side of the building, I said, "Listen, the real reason I was trying to find you is that I found something I thought you'd be interested in reading." He was a big fan of the recent *Cars* movie; I handed him a copy of Disney's *Comic Zone* magazine, which included a section with the characters from the movie.

He looked it over excitedly, thanked me in his own way, and wandered off to his classroom—at least, I suppose that's where he was headed. As I made my way back to the pile of work on my desk, I heard him calling out to me.

"Mr. Thompson, I can't take this with me."

"Why not?" I wondered aloud. "I've got another copy, and you can bring that one back when you're done with it."

"No," he argued, "I mean, I left my backpack at home and don't have any-where to hide this."

Confused, I asked, "Hide it? Why do you need to hide it?"

Appearing just as perplexed as I was, he asked, "Well . . . won't I get in trouble for having it in class?"

This exchange illustrates the fact that comics can be perceived as a forbidden pleasure to many students. Because most adults remain unfamiliar with the medium, and many have yet to fully comprehend the strengths and educational value behind it, graphica is often viewed by students as something only kids get. Giving students a comic is like letting them chew gum in school or play video games during recess. In many schools, it's just not done.

Because it's outside the norm, kids often assume that graphica is prohibited; for many, this makes it all the more enticing and motivating (Kerr and Culhane; Ezarik 2003). This really seems to hold true for my struggling and reluctant readers, who often are more than willing to buck the system. What's more, if you are the adult offering graphica to a student, sometimes that mere act can be enough to create an almost instant relationship with him or her. You're seen as someone who's on the student's side, someone who gets it, someone who's—as we used to say—cool. We mustn't discount the effect these relationships have on our students and their motivation to read and perform.

THE APPEAL OF GRAPHICA

Another reason graphica motivates so many of our learners to read is that it appeals to students from a myriad of different backgrounds, cultures, and per-sonalities (Schwarz 2006). Historically, graphica has been viewed as a medium geared more toward males, but that notion is currently changing as more and more girls become interested in it. It's also been thought to appeal more to middle- and upper-class children, but the truth is that comics know no socio-economic boundaries. In fact, Ujiie and Krashen (1996) studied both middle-class and lower-income students and found no difference in the amount of comic book reading among the subjects.

Michele Gorman offers several reasons that comics appeal to young read-ers, including that they " address current, relevant, often complex social issues such as nonconformity and prejudice as well as themes that are important to young people including coming of age, social injustice, and personal triumph over adversity" (2003, 10). Additionally, the publishing world of graphica has recently taken full advantage of its growing popularity, creating a flurry of titles that offer something of interest to virtually every reader.

LET'S HEAR IT FOR THE BOYS!

It's no secret that comics are skewed toward boys' interests. Admittedly, in the past, comics were mainly written for male readers. Although that trend has shown signs of change, it remains largely in place today. There is a great deal of debate regarding the state of male readers in our educational system. Scholars argue about whether boys are actually more deficient readers than girls overall, or if it's simply a matter of not offering boys something they're motivated to read (Atwell 2007, 94–95; Allington 2005, 9; Lyga 2004, 5-6; Guevara 2006).

I'm limited on time, so I'll leave that debate to more studious folk than myself. I have a job to do, and that job dictates that I take a look at my own students in my own classroom. In doing so, I tend to fall on the side of the fence that argues that boys can, in fact, read just as well as their female counterparts—they just choose not to. I propose that, if we were to suggest literature that they find valuable or worth the effort, they would read up a storm. I believe that many literacy experts would agree with me on this, but again I argue that you have to consider your own little group of readers. Look around your classroom. Do your boys read on level but often misbehave or appear completely lost or uninterested during reading time? Are they less apt to pick up a book for free reading time? Do they avoid reading like the plague? If so, maybe it's time to consider what you are offering them to read. Since comics often present goofy concepts, supernatural heroes, scary tales, and off-the-wall story lines, they naturally grab the attention of many male readers.

LET THE GIRLS HAVE THEIR SAY!

The common assumption that comics are just for boys is a complete and total misconception. Although comics traditionally were geared to the male reader, and many still are, the multitude of female readers of comics is gaining in numbers (Gorman 2003, 10). This trend seems to have started with the manga craze, which impacted older female readers a few years back (Fallis 2005) and has just begun to trickle down to female readers in the lower grades (Fine 2005). Publishers like Tokyopop and Scholastic are listening to their female consumers who are begging for more material that falls within their areas of interest.

Currently, Tokyopop offers titles like *Barbie, Lilo and Stitch*, and *Totally Spies*, while Papercutz has revived and updated the Nancy Drew series with a fresh, modernized look and new story lines. Scholastic offers the ever-popular Baby-Sitters Club in graphic novel format under their Graphix imprint, and Random House publishes an adorable, original graphic novel series called Babymouse, specifically written for younger girls. (See Appendix D for additional information about comics that appeal to girls.)

Regardless, I would encourage you to check your ideas of what's masculine and what's feminine at the door. I teach many girls who fight for their turn to check out the high-action "boy" comics, and just as many boys who love to read Babymouse (albeit cautiously and hidden behind their desks).

ENGLISH LANGUAGE LEARNERS

Another group of learners to whom graphica speaks are those students who are learning English in addition to their first language. Comics' readership is high in countries outside the United States, and as a result, many of our immigrant students come from cultures in which graphica is already a viable literature option (Freeman 1997; Cart 2005; Cary 2004, 61). High interest and the picture support offered in comics can help encourage students who aren't yet proficient in English to continue reading while learning vocabulary and language at the same time. These students can be frightened by the overwhelming amount of text in traditional literature. They often find that the lessened load of text in comics, combined with picture support, help make the act of making meaning much more manageable (Crawford 2004; ALSC Research and Development Committee 2006; McPherson 2006).

Because conversations in graphica are more authentic, readers can experience real, everyday discourse in English as opposed to the more contrived language found in many basal readers and ELL materials (Williams 1995; Davis 1997; Cary 2004, 33). Additionally, graphica can give ELL students an introduction to and practice in the nuances of the English language, such as culturally specific onomatopoeia, verb tenses, multiple-meaning words, and routine phrases (Davis 1997; *Curriculum Review* 2005; Cary 2004, 33).

If you've ever tried to learn a second language, you'll appreciate this final notion. I know some Spanish, but when people speak to me in Spanish, I constantly have to ask them to slow down (and often wish I could slow them down to a crawl in order to fully grasp what they are saying). Graphica offers a *visual permanence* that allows ELL readers to slow down the process of a conversation in a way that is impossible with film and other types of media. As Gene Yang (2003) puts it, "Time within a comic book progresses only as quickly as the reader moves her eyes across the page. The pace at which information is transmitted is completely determined by the reader."

A wealth of information on using comics with ELL students is currently available, and I make comparatively small mention of it here. However, if you want to learn more about the power of comics to teach English language learners, I highly recommend Stephen Cary's (2004) excellent book on the topic, *Going Graphic: Comics at Work in the Multilingual Classroom*. Of specific interest is Cary's inclusion of more than twenty lessons for classroom use, as well as his illustration of Stephen Krashen's optimal conditions for second language development and how graphica can play a pivotal role in this process (Cary 2004, 12).

PICTURE SUPPORT

When you take a look through a comic book or graphic novel, the first thing you'll likely notice is the artwork. The pictures are amazing, and even the works printed in black and white are still eye-catching—and often downright remarkable. Many students are motivated to read comics initially because the pictures draw them in. The images are enticing, but they also offer assistance to readers who need that extra crutch to support them as they travel through the text. This can increase motivation, engagement, and comprehension while being less threatening (Krashen 2004, 123; Gorman 2003, 11; Lyga 2004, 6-7).

Many comics enthusiasts and researchers discuss the notion that students who've grown up in our visually stimulating culture are drawn to comics because they find the visual representations of the text alluring, comfortable, and engaging (Yang 2003; Behler 2006; Cart 2005; Snowball 2005; George 2003). Furthermore, Lyga (2004) introduces the idea that, because of the changing nature of our information delivery systems, students today have become visually dependent; she calls these young readers "Generation Visual." Lyga discusses the draw that comics can have for these learners and argues that, for these students, "static text on an immobile page isn't just boring and laborious; it's practically alien" (2004, 8). It would appear, then, that graphica has much to offer our students by using pictures and graphic art to motivate them to read and support them in their reading.

ENGAGING CONTENT

After more than a decade of working with struggling readers, I've come to the conclusion that we must address the differences between an active and a passive reader. We must name those differences and teach them to students while encouraging them to monitor whether they are actively reading or passively going through the motions. Numerous scholars, researchers, and writers have noted the engaging power that graphica has to awaken our passive readers to active reading. Gene Yang (2003) argues, "Children have a natural attraction to comics," and Rocco Versaci states, "Reading comic books requires an active though largely subconscious participation on the part of the reader" (2001, 63). Kerr and Culhane point out that "our attention system has a built-in bias for high contrast, novelty, and emotional overtones." They argue that, because comics certainly fit the bill in this regard, they "stimulate active participation and engagement" on the part of the reader, creating a kind of "immediacy that can make attention addicts out of otherwise attention disordered individuals."

Additionally, Stephen Cary states that "for a number of reasons—the humor, heroes, movement, pop culture themes, real-world language, novelty, and, perhaps above all, artwork—comics consistently engage students" (2004, 19). These experts have a point. Kids really get into this! I've seen this engagement occur countless times, especially when students begin to moan as I collect my comics to move on to the next classroom. And, of course, I always have the predictable student or two who will beg to take a copy home.

When we see so many students who either can read but won't or avoid reading altogether because they've experienced so much failure around the task (Allington 2005, 10, 171), it stands to reason that, as an educational institution, we would sit up and take notice of such a motivational medium as graphica. Robin Brenner, webmaster for the excellent comics review website www.noflyingnotights.com, sums up this line of reasoning perfectly when she states that, in addition to our on-level readers, comics offer an attraction to many of our students identified as reluctant readers because "the combination of less text, narrative support from images, and feeling of reading outside the expected canon often relieves the tension of reading expectations for kids who are not natural readers, and lets them learn to be confident and engaged consumers of great stories" (2006).

In his book *What Really Matters for Struggling Readers*, Richard Allington (2005) reminds us of the importance of a reader's level of engagement. He argues that we need to create instruction that encourages "internally motivated" reading activities (56) and that, because our struggling readers often show less enthusiasm for reading and tend to avoid the task in general, our instruction for these readers specifically needs to be engaging and powerful (168-169). Whether it be their less-threatening nature, their entertainment component, or their high-interest topics, comics are engaging. Because they are engaging, they often can perk up our passive readers and offer them the experience of what it feels like to be an active participant in the reading process—a feeling that, regrettably, many of them have never had before.

CHAPTER THREE

A WORD ABOUT THE RESEARCH

I have an investigative personality. When I really get drawn into something, I jump in feet first and dig through it with a fine-tooth comb. It's no wonder, then, that when I first chose to look into using graphica with my students, I marched myself down to our district professional library to explore any available research I could get my hands on regarding the topic. I certainly wanted statistical research, but I also looked for qualitative papers, experiences from teachers in the trenches, and professional opinions from some of our more trusted names in literature. I also wanted to consult the Internet, hoping I'd find postings from real teachers who had tried the medium in their classrooms and were eager to share the results. Erroneously thinking that I was one of only a few people who had stumbled on this unique idea, I pretty much convinced myself on the way to the library that I wouldn't find much—if I found anything at all—so I didn't plan to stay long.

Two hours later, as the media specialist gently reminded me they were closing, I sat at the research computer feeling completely and totally overwhelmed! My initial assumption that I'd not find much information was entirely off base; with a sigh, I resolved myself to the fact that I'd need to make another trip to the library.

Five trips later, I was still researching. In fact, I haven't stopped! There's so much out there, and, as I continue my pursuit, I find new, valuable information on a regular basis. To this day, because new investigations and studies are popping up on an almost daily basis, I don't feel I have an absolute grasp of all the information that's out there about using comics in the classroom. However, though it's by no means definitive, I do have a confident understanding of what we know about graphica that makes it an appropriate and valid form of literature to use in our classrooms.

Rather than inundate you with countless articles and research findings—and believe me, they are countless—I've chosen to highlight the research and works of several scholars who've studied and written about the topic. In doing so, I've condensed much of the research that's out there into more manageable points of interest.

In the second edition of his informative and well-researched text *The Power of Reading*, Stephen Krashen (2004) spends more than fifteen pages reviewing the current, available research about comics. In that overview, he discusses research that concludes that comics:

- are popular (95);
- are linguistically appropriate (109);
- can scaffold students toward more difficult reading (105);
- do not slow reading development (97);
- do not negatively affect language development (110);
- do not negatively affect school achievement (110);
- are not responsible for antisocial behavior (94);
- can be found in a wide variety of levels and difficulty (98).

Krashen also discusses research that shows how the presence of graphica in libraries increases library traffic (108) and that, compared to their non-comic book reading peers, readers of comics:

- read as much as non-comics readers (102);
- read more overall (102);
- read more books (110);
- have more positive attitudes toward reading (110);
- are equal in tests of comprehension, vocabulary, language development, and school achievement (104).

In his book that focuses on second language learners and graphica, Stephen Cary (2004) finds research that mirrors much of what Krashen discovered—specifically, that comics are popular (29, 31) and can be a bridge to heavier reading (29). However, Cary includes additional research:

- Though traditionally geared toward boys' interests, comics are also popular among girls (30).
- Comics can be a valuable tool for working with second language learners and exposing them to the spoken discourse of the English language (32).
- Reading comics doesn't discourage or replace other types of reading (28).
- Comics can be a valuable resource for content learning (27).

Recently, the 2006–2007 Association for Library Service to Children's Research and Development Committee (2006) asked the question: Should graphic novels be considered literature? They presented their conclusions in a well-informed literature review paper that repeats findings regarding comics' popularity and reminds us that they appeal to both boys and girls. The committee reiterates that the use of graphica doesn't replace traditional literacy learning, and includes other interesting information on the subject:

- More graphica is being printed with the elementary-aged student in mind.
- Reading comics may have positive effects on children's cognitive growth.
- Comics offer great practice with using multiple-meaning words.
- Struggling readers are more likely to read comics than traditional texts.
- Reading graphica offers practice in using critical thinking skills.
- Comics can improve motivation to read and thereby improve vocabulary, comprehension, and pleasure reading.

Bear in mind that this summation is just the tip of the literature iceberg regarding the use of graphica in the classroom. Nonetheless, if you've been around the mulberry bush enough times, you've probably learned to take educational "research" with a grain of salt. If you're still skeptical, I encourage you to take some time to mull this section over. Reread it, and follow up with the references I've listed. Make it make sense for you. Ultimately, you will use what works in your classroom and what fits the needs of your students. I'm convinced that, once you give it a try, you will be pleasantly surprised at how graphica can work wonders for you and your kiddos.

CHAPTER FOUR

INTRODUCING THE CONVENTIONS OF GRAPHICA

Although kids take to graphica with little trouble, there are some things you'll want to explicitly show them—that is, of course, if they don't figure them out on their own first. Many of your students may already be familiar with comics and will need little or no introduction, whereas others may have only a passing knowledge (or no knowledge at all) of the medium and will need you to help them break it down. Whether comics are a new guest in your classroom or simply new to a few of your students, an introduction will be in order.

LAYOUT AND ORGANIZATIONAL FORMATS

Introducing the layout and organizational formats of different types of texts is an essential part of our regular literacy instruction. For example, when we teach students about nonfiction, we notice and teach its conventions, such as captions, time lines, graphs, subheadings, diagrams, and more. The same holds true for graphica. You'll want to show students that, when they read comics, knowing about the various conventions the writers and artists use and why they use them can help them understand the meaning of the text. Let's take a look at the general conventions of graphica that you'll want to show your students.

LAYOUT

The first thing you and your students will notice about graphica is the way it is organized. Graphica takes a complete U-turn from the layout of traditional texts. At first glance, it seems to break all the rules—and I think this is one of the reasons it appeals to students. The layout is all about visual attendance; it requires readers to divide their attention among a whole host of different things going on across the page. Luckily, the transition to this new design is one most students make without hesitation.

PANELS

The progression of the information or story in comics occurs through a series of panels that is analogous to paragraphing in traditional texts. Sometimes called *frames*, these panels link together in a cumulative, puzzle-like manner to create the meaning of the piece as a whole. Placement, size, and action within these panels are used strategically to move the piece along. Although the panels are often presented as squares and rectangles, different creative teams may render them in various shapes or contours as they lend themselves to maintaining the meaning of the text.

SPEECH BUBBLES

Dialogue in comics is mainly represented using speech bubbles. These are, perhaps, the most recognizable feature of comics. A variation of these can be seen in thought bubbles, which represent the characters' thinking and are generally depicted as cloud-shaped speech bubbles. Artists use different styles of speech bubbles in accordance with the mood or meaning of the panel. For example, a wavy speech bubble may be used to indicate that the character is frightened, or a jagged-edge speech bubble may represent the electronic voice of a robot or an answering machine.

NARRATIVE BOXES

Narrative boxes, which often appear as narrow text boxes near the top or bottom of the panel, can serve many purposes. They can act as an offshoot of the traditional speech bubble, specifically if one of the characters is serving as the narrator of the story. These text boxes are also used when the piece is narrated in the third person. Narrative boxes might additionally note the setting or alert the reader that something in the time line is changing (for example, "Later that same day in Metropolis . . ."). Narrative boxes are often used to summarize one or more panels, thereby continuing to help the reader maintain meaning.

LETTERING

Lettering in graphica is often cleverly used to create mood or to offer the reader assistance with phrasing or intonation. For instance, boldface words should be stressed, whereas words written with smaller letters might be deemphasized. Teachers are often surprised to find that most traditional comics are written in all capital letters and only veer from that pattern to emphasize a point or to support meaning (for example, using all lowercase lettering to indicate that a character is whispering). At first, this feature may seem like it would confuse readers, but most students breeze right past it with no trouble. However, if this is a concern for you, don't fret. Recently, some publishers that produce graphica specifically for younger children have begun to use both uppercase and lowercase lettering in the traditional way throughout their works.

DIRECTIONALITY

Graphica is read from left to right and top to bottom, just like traditional texts. Creators may veer from this pattern at times to draw readers to something specific or because it is a more effective way to support the meaning of the text. The directionality, speech bubbles, and panels in comics are extremely meaning driven; if the reader takes a wrong turn on the page, the meaning immediately begins to break down.

IMPORTANCE OF THE PICTURES

Even when traditional forms of literature use pictures to support the text, most maintain a definite physical division between the two. Not so with comics! The artwork in graphica is important to the piece as a whole and plays an intricate part in the delivery of the text's content. The words are ingrained in the pictures. In fact, the two are inseparable.

It is important for students to know that the graphics and text work together to help the reader make meaning. Since this explanation can be difficult for younger elementary students to understand, I usually simplify it by saying, "The pictures and words are married! They go everywhere together!" For more sophisticated students, I may offer a deeper explanation by discussing how the writers and illustrators work together to tell the story. We discuss how they think about everything—the words and the art—that will help tell the story *before* they put it on the page. We seal our understanding with a catchphrase that we refer back to often: "It's not there for pretty—everything on the page is important!"

When students become more sophisticated in their understanding of graphica, you'll want to spend a lot of time exploring the dynamic, interdependent relationship between the pictures and the text. But as you introduce the medium, students only need to understand that you can't *just* read the words or *just* look at the pictures. Graphica simply doesn't work that way. You have to do both. Children learning about comics should be taught that, because the pictures hold the meaning of the story (just like in the books they learned to read with), effective readers of graphica should spend a while on the pictures and consider their ramifications on the story line or information being delivered. The pictures hold power. They're not there for pretty!

THE GUTTER

I was completely oblivious to the gutter before a group of my students taught me. In actuality, we learned together. During independent reading time a few years ago, a group of my third graders asked if they could share a Spider-Man comic book. Although four students to one book isn't a ratio I'd usually support for our independent reading block, they seemed eager. After a quick debate, we agreed—but only on the condition that they would stay on task with their sharing and thinking, without behavioral problems. They agreed and seemed completely committed to following through, but I had my doubts. About ten minutes later, a commotion began to brew in their reading area. I quickly ended the conference I was holding with another student and stormed over. "What is going on over here? I thought we had a deal?"

"We do," the bravest one answered, "but we're stuck!"

"Stuck? What do you mean?"

The only girl in the group countered, "Well, we don't know what happened to Spider-Man! He was there, and now he's not!" The rest of the group nodded in agreement, bewildered and perplexed.

"Help me understand what you mean when you say you don't know what happened to Spider-Man," I requested. They showed me the page they were reading and explained their confusion. In one panel, Spider-Man somersaulted into the top of a huge bush. The next panel showed a man walking down the street, wearing a backpack. Spider-Man, it appeared, was nowhere to be found.

Referring to the mini-lesson I had taught earlier about inferring, I encouraged the students to look for clues in the text and pictures to figure out what happened. We discussed the man with the backpack and checked the next few panels as he walked into Aunt Mae's house and helped himself to a piece of pie. One student wondered about the backpack, while the quietest of the four reminded us that Peter Parker, Spider-Man's secret identity, lived with Aunt Mae (and that we should have known that because "everyone knows that"). In a matter of moments, and almost simultaneously, the students were able to deduce on their own that, apparently, Spider-Man had changed his clothes in the bushes, put them in his backpack, and walked home as Peter Parker, because he didn't want Aunt Mae to find out that he was really Spider-Man.

This led us to a discussion of the white space in between the frames. As we read on, we noticed that a lot happens to the plot of a comic within that white space that the reader is left to infer. Our learning that day was so powerful, I let those students lead our mini-lesson the next day based on what we'd learned. Not knowing any better, we called the white space the "ditch." In time, research would lead me to the official term for this feature: the *gutter*.

If you aren't paying close attention, the influence of the gutter might escape you. It's so subtle, and so much a part of the graphica layout, that most proficient readers glide past it without noticing. The gutter doesn't stand out, but, like the mortar between the bricks of a house, it holds the entire comic together. Scott McCloud (1993) devotes an entire chapter to the nuances and power of the gutter in his book *Understanding Comics: The Invisible Art*. At one point, he uses the analogy that the gutters are essentially the veins through which the life of the comic flows (73).

Once students understand the way the gutter works, it can be used as a natural checkpoint from which to direct and shore up their thinking. Each gutter can be used as a placeholder, as children add to their cumulative understanding of the piece. Gutters offer a wide variety of instructional possibilities—many of which we'll revisit later—and can be used to predict and anticipate the next panels, make connections, clarify confusion, ask questions, make inferences, and draw conclusions.

TEACHING THE CONVENTIONS OF GRAPHICA

When teaching graphica, as with traditional texts, we must explicitly teach text conventions if we want our students to find success in formats that are new to them. Depending on the needs of your class, this initial, explicit instruction can be done individually or in small or whole-class groups. I usually prefer to introduce comics to the whole class at once, because the shared experience seems to enhance classroom cohesiveness. Besides, when I try to do so with a small group or an individual, others in the class become so intrigued that they eventually start to wonder—and ask—if they are going to "get to read those" too. Case in point: once, a third-grade teacher called my office, asking me what I planned to do about "this epidemic" I'd caused in her classroom. I could hear the frustration in her voice as she explained that, since I'd given one of her struggling students a comic, her whole class wouldn't stop begging for their own comics. Unsure of exactly how to respond, I offered, "Well, I suppose I could bring enough for everyone. . . ." She calmly answered, "I think that's what they were hoping for!"

Regardless of the grouping format you choose, I suggest you introduce graphica in the same way that you might teach a classic genre study lesson—with plenty of exploration and discussion—except that, with graphica, you will essentially be doing a *medium* study rather than a *genre* study. This is the same way I introduce other forms of literature, such as magazines, poetry, and newspapers. Because it's fun and hands-on, my students really seem to get more out of it. The following introduction focuses on the conventions of graphica discussed earlier in this chapter and can be taught in two lessons. The first is an investigative experience, and the second is a follow-up lesson meant to clarify and summarize the learning.

LESSON 1

In this first lesson, I invite students to investigate the way graphica works and then give them opportunities to explore it further. But, be warned! You'll likely have a riot on your hands if you introduce comics to a group of children and then forget to leave enough time for them to enjoy the medium on their own. As you plan to repeat this lesson with your kiddos, remember to schedule ample independent reading time toward the end that allows students a chance to have a personal experience with graphica.

To begin the lesson, I put a pile of comics in the middle of our circle and ask everyone to help themselves to a few selections. I lead the students in a discussion of what they already know about comics and what previous experiences they've had with them. This can be done orally or as a written survey (see Figure 4.1), though I find the oral discussion much more powerful. Most students will know that comics are printed in black and white as well as color. A few will be able to tell you the names of the characters in the more popular titles, and still others will make personal connections to some of their favorite movies. Most students expect the medium to be funny and entertaining, with lots of action. Interestingly, almost all students (erroneously) assume that all graphica is fiction—a common misconception even among adults. We continue our discussion until everyone who wants to share has had a chance to do so.

Comics!

Take a few minutes to think about comics. Then write down what you know or think you know about them.

I think that comics are the best things to read when you're having fun. It's cool because each little or big square has every scene of what's happening in the Action. Either its Captain Underpants or some other hero Type, I think it's the BEST.

FIG 4.1 Brandon's written response to the question, "What do you already know about comics?"

Next, I allow students to read and explore their selections with their pair/share partners or in small groups. As they examine their samples, I ask them to jot down what they notice. Depending on the sophistication of the students, I use either conversation or a written questionnaire (see Figure 4.2) to guide their thinking with specific inquiries:

What did you notice?
How is it organized?
How is it like other mediums, formats, or genres we've studied?
How is it different?
What do you like about it?
What do you not like about it?

Example Responses to Exploration Guide Questions

What did you notice?
    "It looks fake, and it has lots of colors."
    "It takes longer to read than it looks like it will!"
    "Scanning the pictures is a good preview to the story line."
    "Plenty of action!"
    "It has talking bubbles."

"It has lots of color."

"Ours has chapters!"

How is it organized?

"It is made with squares and rectangles."

"Your eyes go left to right and then straight down."

"Your eyes go back and forth (showing left to right with finger)."

How is it like other mediums, formats, or genres we've studied?

"Ours is fiction (superheroes)."

"My pile has fantasy and fiction."

"Mine has informational text."

"Mine is realistic fiction."

"Ours is historical fiction."

How is it different from other mediums, formats, or genres we've studied?

"There are no paragraphs!"

"Ours has pictures and speech bubbles in boxes instead of paragraphs."

What do you like about it?

"I like that it is very illustrated."

"My favorite has characters with superpowers!"

"Ours has real reading with kid stuff."

"It makes us want to learn more!"

"It has less words than a regular book."

"Mine has some of my favorite shows (Disney's *Comic Zone*)."

"We think it is interesting to us."

What do you not like about it?

"The words in our book might be too easy."

"It's cartoonish."

"I like everything about it!"

"Nothing—we think this book is awesome!"

Next, we discuss their responses. During this conversational exploration, students generally hit on many of the major conventions of graphica that they need to be aware of, without my help. I summarize their findings and give them the

Katheline and Joanae

Exploring Comics: Getting Started

With your partner/group, take a look at the text you were given and discuss the following
questions. Come back to sharing time prepared to discuss your answers.

1. What do you notice?

we noticed pictures are
black and white and
there's lots of
colors, too.

2. How is it organized?

It's organized in
boxes and squres.

3. How is it like other resources we've studied?

Because one is fiction
and the other one
is realistic fiction.

4. How is it different than other resources we've studied?

Because the other books
we've studied are in
paragraghs and comics
are in boxes and speech
bubblies.

5. What do you like about it?

Because it has
less words than
a regearer book.

6. What do you not like about it?

we like every thing
about it.

FIG 4.2 Katheline and Joanae's written responses to the graphica survey

correct terms for the features they've noticed. If any of the conventions require
further explanation, we cover them, and then I end the lesson by allowing a good
chunk of independent reading time in which to further explore the medium.
While doing so, I ask students to continue to share their thinking about the

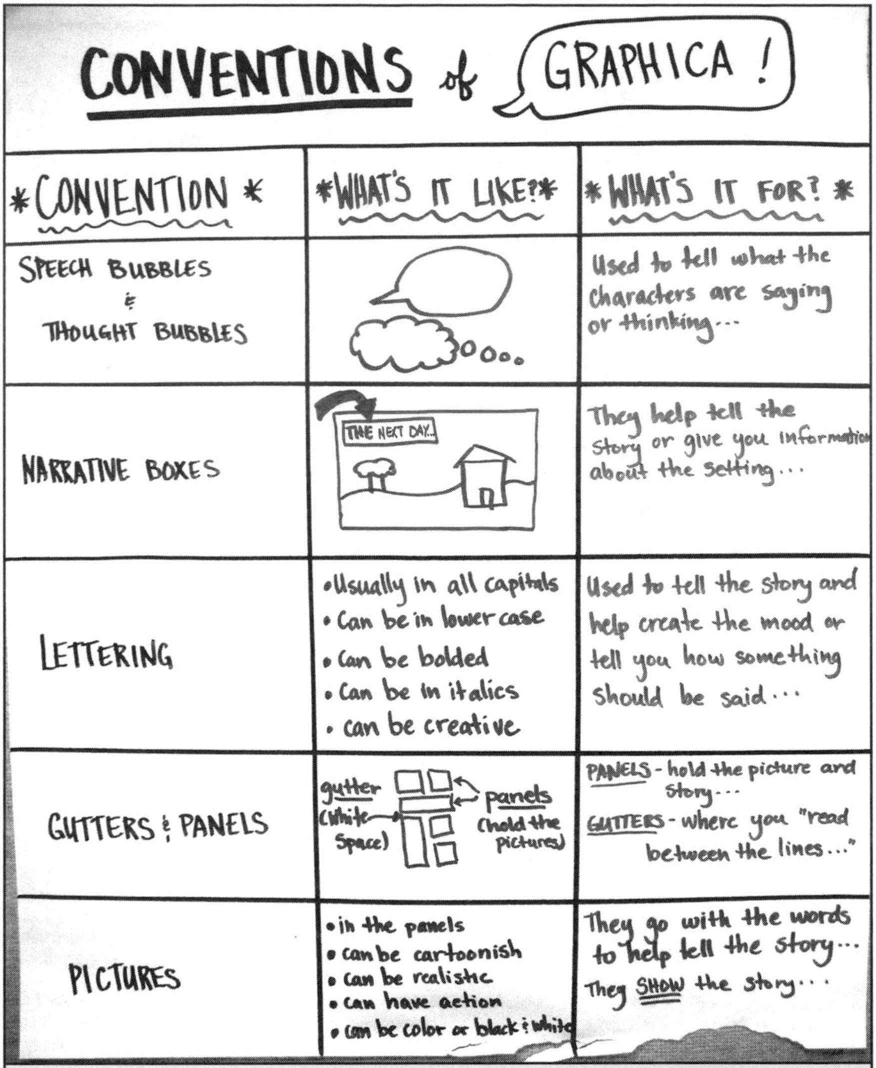

CONVENTIONS of **GRAPHICA !**

CONVENTION	*WHAT'S IT LIKE?*	*WHAT'S IT FOR?*
SPEECH BUBBLES & THOUGHT BUBBLES		Used to tell what the characters are saying or thinking...
NARRATIVE BOXES	THE NEXT DAY...	They help tell the story or give you information about the setting...
LETTERING	• Usually in all capitals • Can be in lower case • Can be bolded • Can be in italics • can be creative	Used to tell the story and help create the mood or tell you how something should be said...
GUTTERS & PANELS	gutter (white space) panels (hold the pictures)	PANELS - hold the picture and story... GUTTERS - where you "read between the lines..."
PICTURES	• in the panels • can be cartoonish • Can be realistic • can have action • can be color or black & white	They go with the words to help tell the story... They SHOW the story...

FIG 4.3 "Conventions of Graphica" anchor chart created with a group of third graders

medium in their reading response journals. When we come back to the floor for sharing time, we review and summarize our thoughts by beginning an anchor chart titled "Conventions of Graphica," which includes some of the major concepts brought up during the lesson (see Figure 4.3).

LESSON 2

In the next lesson, I bring the students together and attempt to fill in the gaps left from the previous lesson by pinpointing certain conventions the students may have missed that I want to ensure they understand clearly. I might also highlight features that they noticed in the previous lesson but need to dwell on a bit more thoroughly. The goal of this follow-up lesson is to merge those conventions of graphica that the students discovered during their initial exploration with the ones I feel that they need to know about to fluently navigate comics without losing the meaning. Students are then given a large block of time to read comics on their own. When we return to the floor for sharing, we complete the anchor chart we started in the first lesson by adding the important conventions we discussed during this lesson.

• • •

After these initial introductory lessons, most students are bursting at the seams to start reading comics, and this may be all you have to do to add graphica to the literacy culture of your classroom. If, however, you find that your learners need a more detailed understanding of the medium, your follow-up lessons could include a series of deeper discussions about the individual conventions listed earlier in the chapter. Additionally, should you find that the group needs more hands-on practice, you could plan subsequent lessons that offer opportunities to search for and chart examples of these conventions in other graphica titles.

CHAPTER FIVE

ENDLESS POSSIBILITIES FOR USING GRAPHICA

Once comics are firmly planted in your classroom, you'll find a variety of ways to use them. Locating multiple copies of a title is an easy process, and, once you have them, you can use them for guided reading (see Figure 5.1) or strategy focus groups. Want to spice up your literature circles? Consider offering a round that's based on graphica (see Figure 5.2). In either instance, you'll quickly notice that students react positively to the experience.

Can you use comics to conduct read-alouds and think-alouds? Sure you can, but I'll admit that it can be a bit tricky. You'll want to consider the text you are choosing as well as your audience. Students have to know what's going on in the pictures, or they quickly lose interest. Primary students need to see the pictures clearly, whereas intermediate students can make due with a clear description of what's happening from the reader. As you read, you can describe the action in the picture and add identifiers to who's speaking, pointing out the picture and the corresponding speech bubble as you do so. *Don't Let the Pigeon Drive the Bus!* by Mo Willems is one of my favorite read-alouds (see Figure 5.3), because the pictures and the text are large enough for the entire class to see. Its simplistic layout also gives everyone ample opportunity to attend to the text's meaning.

If your selection has a lot for the reader to monitor, consider using an overhead copy of the text or a document camera so students can see the pictures. Only a few graphica-based big books and teaching posters exist at this point, so you could use this same setup to lead shared reading opportunities (see Figure 5.4).

FIG 5.1   The author leads a first-grade guided reading group using Red Brick Learning's *Eek and Ack: Invaders from the Great Goo Galaxy.*

FIG 5.2   A literature circle group reads graphica.

FIG 5.3   Elaine Hallford leads a read-aloud of *Don't Let the Pigeon Drive the Bus!* with her first graders.

FIG 5.4   The author leads a shared reading lesson.

FIG 5.5 In this classroom library, comics are displayed among all of the other independent reading options.

In both instances, be sure to stop along the way to visit the pictures and discuss the role they play in the reading process.

Graphica incorporates easily into the reading workshop. After you introduce comics to the class, all you need to do is make sure that students have them as options during their independent reading time (see Figure 5.5), and offer mini-lessons from time to time that feature the medium—especially when comics lend themselves to your traditional lessons.

You'll also find a lot of opportunities to incorporate graphica into your writing lessons and discussions. When one of Mindy Butler's ELL students, Danny, was struggling with learning to write a personal narrative, she and I decided to capitalize on his affinity for graphica. You see, Danny was completely enamored with comics and had even been writing his own for some time. Mindy successfully coached him to use his skills at creating comics to sketch out the small moments of his narrative during the planning stages of his writing. She taught Danny to use those sketches as a map from which to write his personal narrative. This was the first step of a real growing period in Danny's writing.

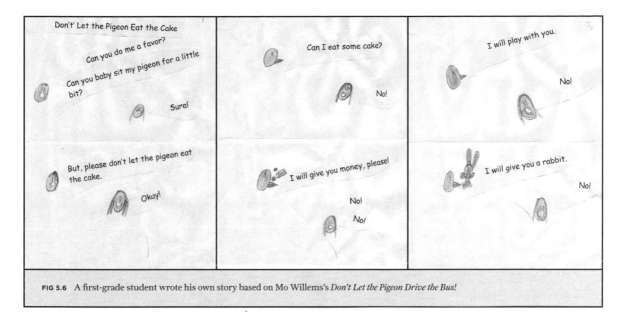

FIG 5.6   A first-grade student wrote his own story based on Mo Willems's *Don't Let the Pigeon Drive the Bus!*

In another instance, after reading aloud from Mo Willems's *Don't Let the Pigeon Drive the Bus!*, Elaine Hallford's first-grade students decided to write their own versions of the book (see Figure 5.6). They even tried their hand at using speech bubbles to indicate dialogue. This isn't unusual. In fact, as students start to explore graphica, you'll often find that many naturally make the jump to writing their own comics without you even having to suggest it!

It's true that comics are an exceptional tool for literacy development, but you'll soon find them flowing over into your content areas as well. More and more teachers have begun to integrate their literature and content area instructional blocks. And well they should! But even without the obvious literacy connection, comics can help illustrate many other instructional areas by engaging students in visual representations of content vocabulary, historical events, and scientific concepts, just to name a few (see Figure 5.7). Savvy teachers will be on the lookout for titles that lend themselves to these areas. Be sure to check out Appendix E, "Publishers Offering Graphica," for the names of some publishers who release titles based in content areas.

FIG 5.7 Students use Rosen Classroom's graphic nonfiction series, Graphic Battles of the Civil War, as part of their social studies lesson.

MOVING FROM GRAPHICA TO TRADITIONAL TEXT

In Chapter 3, I mentioned research that discusses how reading comics can serve as a conduit to heavier reading and even greater instances of reading traditional texts. For the most part, this is a natural by-product of reading comics and will happen even without our help. However, because I am not willing to accept mere happenstance, part of my work with graphica has included a hunt for different ways to help this process along. My search has led me to two unique methods that you might find useful in transitioning readers from comics to traditional texts: "bridge comics" and "paired concept reading."

BRIDGE COMICS

A great way to encourage readers of comics to dip their toes into the waters of traditional texts is to introduce them to what I call bridge comics (I can't seem to find the proper name for this, and maybe it doesn't exist—I may have just coined a new phrase!). Essentially, bridge comics operate by alternating comics and conventional literature within the same story line, allowing the graphica format

FINDING BRIDGE COMICS

Want to explore some good bridge comics? Check out the starter list of bridge comics in Appendix D, "Suggested Titles."

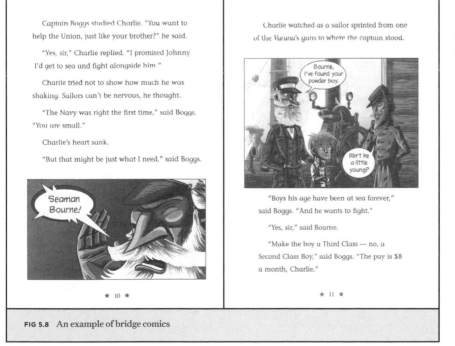

FIG 5.8   An example of bridge comics

to work as a sort of training wheel that helps readers shift into traditional texts more comfortably.

Figure 5.8 is an example of this format from Red Brick Learning's *Hot Iron: The Adventures of a Civil War Powder Boy*. Notice how the graphica format coordinates with pockets of traditional text to create the story. The panels pick up the story line and carry it forward. Then, when it's time, they seamlessly steer the story right back into the traditional text layout. This format is great because it's win-win: it captures the attention of readers who love comics and propels them forward through traditional text, and it keeps them reading with perfectly timed placements of graphica panels along the way. In my opinion, bridge comics hold great potential because they pair the draw and engagement of comics with the exposure and practice found in traditional texts—the best of both worlds!

PAIRED CONCEPT READING

PAIRED CONCEPT READING FOR UPPER GRADES

Steck-Vaughn recently introduced a new series called Lynx. In these sets, the company offers pairs of titles—one in graphica format and the other in traditional format—that focus on the same science or social studies concept. See Appendix E, "Publishers Offering Graphica," for more information.

Another way to move readers from comics to traditional texts involves pairing graphica titles with non-graphica counterparts that have the same theme or concept. Fans of graphica could start by reading the comic version of a topic, and then read about the same concept in traditional format. Reading the graphica format first will, no doubt, be engaging and familiar to the student, but it will also offer a fair amount of visual support and background knowledge that the student can use when he or she reads about the topic in the traditional text. For instance, I might start graphica readers off with Rosen Classroom's Graphic Natural Disasters: *Hurricanes* and then encourage them to read a traditional nonfiction text such as *The Weather Channel Presents: Hurricanes!* Depending on the direction I'm taking with the instruction, I could even pair it with David Wiesner's fiction trade book *Hurricane*, a story about a family's personal experiences when a hurricane blows into town.

Another way paired concept reading can work is by offering different adaptations of titles together. Sometimes, the comics your students read are offshoots of a traditional chapter book series, and we can take advantage of their interest in the graphica format to introduce them to the original work. For example, if you've got readers who are hooked on the high-interest Nancy Drew manga imprint from Papercutz, I bet you wouldn't have to twist their arms to get them to try a traditional Nancy Drew chapter book.

By the way, it isn't unusual for this to work the other way around, with a tried-and-true comic being adapted into a trade book or novel. Do you have readers who are huge fans of DC Comics for Kids' Batman titles? Try transitioning them into Scholastic Readers' Batman chapter books. Popular characters from comics are always popping up in traditional picture books and chapter books, and these titles are usually easy to locate at your local bookstore.

TRANSLATE THE TRANSFER

As your students begin to gain a working knowledge of the way graphica works, it's just a hop, skip, and a jump to using the medium to your advantage. In time, you'll discover how strategically used graphica can significantly boost various areas of instruction throughout your teaching day. Because the medium lures students in, you'll find that many of them pay closer attention to lessons that involve graphica. Once they are hooked, all you'll have to do is simply *translate the transfer*.

To me, the concept of "translating the transfer" is possibly the most valuable advantage that comics can offer our teaching. With very few exceptions, you can use graphica to make the concepts you normally teach students in traditional texts concrete and tangible.

The crafty teacher will take advantage of the fact that the layout of graphica motivates and engages students. Even as students think they are merely having fun, you will be laying the seeds for future instruction. As we are intentional in planning and instruction, we can think forward to future references we will make to current lessons. Then we can say, "Do you remember what we did with that comic we looked at last week? Well, you can do the same thing here!"

For example, while discussing the need for students to "read between the lines" in a traditional chapter book, I might return to the discussion we had about Spider-Man in the bushes (mentioned in Chapter 4). I could say, "Guys, think back to when we learned about the gutters in that comic book we read last month. Do you remember how there was a lot going on in that white space, and how we had to really think about it and use clues to figure it out on our own? Well, you can do the same thing here, in between the paragraphs of this chapter book, *just like you did in the comic book gutters*. The book is different, but the job is the same. If you can do it in comics, you can do it here. Let's try it together!"

Throughout the remainder of this book, be on the lookout for different ways the lessons and discussions lend themselves to translating the transfer. I'll point them out along the way, but don't rely on me. I find new ways to do this every day, and there's no doubt you'll come up with some of your own that I haven't even thought of. Just remember: if they can do it with comics, they can do it with traditional texts!

CHAPTER SIX

COMPREHENSION, COMICALLY

Comprehension is the art of the invisible. When readers make meaning of text, it's a silent, internal process. As a result, the structures and nuances of comprehension can be downright difficult to teach. I don't know about you, but I've often wished for my own magic school bus, so that I could shrink myself down and forage through my readers' minds to see what they are thinking. Or, better yet, so I could take my entire class on a field trip inside the mind of a more proficient reader in order to see firsthand what it looks like to make meaning while reading. Imagine how much easier our jobs would be!

Of course, we can't do that—but we try our best, don't we? We carefully tailor our lessons in ways that help us illustrate for students what readers do in their heads while they read, and we engage in conversations with children to better understand their thinking. We study professional books like *Mosaic of Thought*, *Strategies That Work*, *Reading with Meaning*, and countless others that support us in this endeavor by naming choice comprehension strategies and showing us how to bring them to light in our daily literacy lessons. We know that, as they read, proficient readers monitor their comprehension, make connections to the text, create mental images, draw inferences, generate questions, determine what's important, and synthesize their reading. We strive to make these strategies visible to our students in various ways, and we're getting better at it all the time. However, despite our most diligent observations of oral reading and our most in-depth conferences with our students, sometimes the best we can do is make educated guesses about what's going on in their minds as they read. Even

COMPREHENSION STRATEGIES

For more information on comprehension strategy instruction, see:

• *Mosaic of Thought*, 2nd edition by Keene and Zimmermann (Heinemann, 2007)
• *Strategies That Work*, 2nd edition by Harvey and Goudvis (Stenhouse, 2007)
• *Reading with Meaning* by Miller (Stenhouse, 2002)
• *Starting with Comprehension* by Cunningham and Shagoury (Stenhouse, 2005)

as we use mini-lessons, read-alouds, and think-alouds to make good comprehension strategies more tangible to students, they often remain invisible.

Graphica, on the other hand, is the art of the visible—graphic representations of meaning are part of its very nature. As I mentioned in Chapter 4, the symbiotic relationship between the text and the pictures is central to graphica. The pictures are the pillars that support meaning making, and we can use this visibility to our advantage as we attempt to make comprehension strategies obvious in our instruction. In this way, comics can be another tool in our toolbox that helps make the invisible visible—for both instructional and assessment purposes.

In this chapter and the next—for the sake of simplicity—we'll look at each comprehension strategy individually. This chapter will discuss the following strategies:

Monitoring
Synthesizing
Making Connections
Questioning
Determining Importance

Chapter 7 will cover the remaining two strategies:

Making Mental Images
Inferring

As we visit each strategy, we'll look at the ways that working with graphica can fortify its instruction. Despite this organizational technique, please know that in no way do I mean to imply that these strategies occur in isolation during the process of reading. Rather, they work as a team—each one's influence adds to the other, simultaneously supporting comprehension.

MOTIVATION, INTEREST, AND ENGAGEMENT

. . . for many students, the largest steps along the road to literacy are often self-motivated and driven by a need to pursue one's bliss, fire, passion, addiction, interest, joy, or other engaging endeavor of one's choosing.

KEITH MCPHERSON, "Graphic Literacy"

A discussion of comprehension wouldn't be complete if we didn't take into account the value of motivation, interest, and engagement. Powerful comprehension instruction stimulates these traits in its learners. Without them, our lessons lag and lose their effectiveness.

Think of something that you desperately wanted to do in your own life that, without motivation, you might not have otherwise accomplished. For me, it was refinishing an old chair from our church rummage sale. Even though I had never done any type of furniture work before, I was determined to figure it out. I spent countless hours working in the garage and wrestled with more than a few moments of severe frustration. But in the end, I persevered, turning a puke-green eyesore into a wonderful work of art. (Well, to me it's art. Never mind the fact that the upholstery bunches a little and emits a squeaking noise as it gently slides its occupant onto the floor, leaving me with a delightful chair that no one will sit on.) Despite the fact that it didn't turn out perfectly, I love that little chair and remain proud of the effort I put into it.

Now let's move from the chair to the classroom. Motivation and engagement are just as vital when we consider our readers' comprehension. In *What Really Matters for Struggling Readers,* Richard Allington reminds us that "when motivation and interest are low, we often simply terminate the reading activity—sometimes with obvious symptoms of frustration" (2005, 89). As students learn to think about their thinking, they need texts that intrigue them and make them anxious to read. Here's where graphica can play an important role. I once consulted with a teacher who was concerned that one of her literature circle groups had chosen a comic that seemed a bit too difficult for them, and we brainstormed ways she could help. After visiting with the group, however, we both realized that the students were so enthusiastic about reading the text that they were planning to push through it, come what may. We agreed that it would be best to let the group continue, but we decided to monitor them more closely along the way. In the end, the students were able to complete the text with a successful understanding of the story line. It took a bit more work on their parts, but the kids didn't seem to mind at all. In fact, they seemed to enjoy it. Motivation and engagement are powerful forces. Because of its novelty—and its engaging text and pictures—graphica often motivates readers even when other texts fail to do so.

MONITORING AND CLARIFYING

About a year ago, Laurie, a workshop participant, shared with me that she had come to hear my presentation because she was intrigued by what her friend had learned about the power of graphica at a previous workshop I had given. Laurie explained to me that her fourteen-year-old daughter suffered from mild dyslexia and refused to read unless she had to, and she wondered if perhaps her daughter could be enticed to read comics. After the workshop, Laurie took home some comics. She had intended to put them on the coffee table and just watch to see how her kids would respond, but they never even made it to the table. Before she had a chance to put the comics out, her daughter picked up one of the titles and read the entire thing from start to finish. In her email to me the next day, Laurie excitedly wrote: "She even commented to her brother while reading that she would have never read the book, even though it was a topic of great interest to her, if it hadn't been in comic form. We talked when she had finished, and I told her that I noticed her rereading and monitoring her comprehension. She said, 'No, Mom. I got lost and was trying to make sense of the story!'"

Proficient readers monitor the meaning of what they read. They notice when something goes awry and take immediate steps to fix it. They reread to clarify confusions and, in the process, add to the ultimate meaning they take away from the text. In the second edition of *Strategies That Work*, Stephanie Harvey and Anne Goudvis write, "In the years since we wrote *Strategies That Work*, we began to see that teaching kids to monitor their understanding before focusing on specific strategies made all of the difference" (2007, 4). Graphica lends itself perfectly to practice in monitoring meaning. The natural and intricate way its artwork, panels, speech bubbles, and lettering work together to steer the reader to the meaning is nothing short of a literary ballet. This is deliberately done to support comprehension; as Allyson and Barry Lyga write, "A well-designed comic book page will lead the reader naturally from one word balloon to the next, one caption to the next, one panel to the next" (2004, 20). Readers are entranced as the graphics and the words work together, visually moving across the page to create meaning.

Perhaps it's best if I illustrate this for you. Take a moment to study the page from Marvel Age's *Spider-Man #8* in Figure 6.1 and note how the creative team uses everything at its disposal to support the reader in monitoring the meaning of the text.

Allow me to walk you through it. The scene begins at the top left and follows the traditional left-to-right direction to get the reader started. Notice how the second and third panels are connected by a continuation speech bubble to alert us that, although Spider-Man is shown, Electro is still speaking. Notice as

FIG 6.1

well that, even as it does this, we are propelled into the next panel. As the row of panels follows the traditional return sweep into the fourth panel, something strange happens: the story seems to stop. Or does it? Take special note of how the second speech bubble in the fourth panel—"Spider-Man!"—hangs off the panel, just slightly to the right, and forces us into the spread in the middle of the page. As our brain begins to search for the next logical step, our eyes almost naturally fall on the appropriate speech bubble, strategically placed under the previous one. When we finish reading Electro's threat, our eyes notice that his hand is outstretched and lightning bolts are shooting out of it. As our brains and eyes follow those lightning bolts, along with the onomatopoeia ("SHRAKT!"), we find Spider-Man upside down and flying through the air as a result of the attack. The particular way that Spider-Man hangs in the air pairs with the way Electro's lightning bolts leap outward to push our attention into the last panel, where the speech bubbles containing Spider-Man's counterthreat hang just inside the panel and direct our attention to his final attack.

Whew! There's more going on than you thought, right? When you break it down, it does seem like a lot—and, truthfully, it is. However, writing teams are so intentional about this feature that, when they do it well, it's seamless.

I don't suggest that you break down every page with students this way. Please don't. For one thing, you really don't need to—kids take to this naturally. That's the beauty of the way graphica guides readers to monitor their comprehension. They find it appealing and supportive, and they quickly develop an automaticity for navigating through it. For another thing, if it doesn't work for them, if they take a wrong turn somewhere, students quickly notice that something's out of whack. Because they're more motivated than usual, they tend to backtrack quickly to find out where they went wrong and make attempts to fix it, using the plentiful visual clues along the way. What's more, they don't seem to mind the extra work involved. Perhaps it's because they're so engaged, but many young readers seem more willing to do this fix-up work in comics than anywhere else. They don't even notice it. Lucky for us, while they're not noticing it, they're getting a lot of practice in monitoring comprehension.

TRANSLATE THE TRANSFER

When students become proficient in monitoring meaning within graphica, you can remind them to do the same in traditional text. "You know how, when you lose your place in a comic book and it doesn't make sense, you have to go back to figure out where you got lost? So you check the other panels and reread sections until you're on the right track again? Well, you can do that with other types of reading too–in a chapter book, for instance. If you get lost, take a minute and review the other paragraphs to see where your meaning broke down, and reread a few until you are back on track."

MONITORING FOR SHIFTS

When readers lose the meaning in traditional texts, it's often because they aren't prepared for a change that's about to happen. How often have you conferred with a student who, while reading a traditional text, lost the meaning because the dialogue got confusing, the setting changed all of a sudden, or the author included a memory sequence? In graphica, these shifts are represented visually by the artwork, which serves as a guiding device. It notifies readers that things are changing and helps them monitor their reading. Whereas transitions between speakers and settings are more obvious (we can actually *see* them), flashbacks and dream sequences are often visually represented through an alteration of the coloring and drawings. For example, in Figure 6.2, taken from *Babymouse: Queen of the World*, notice how Jennifer and Matthew Holm choose to illustrate Babymouse's daydreams by shading the background. As Babymouse begins to fantasize about being the Queen of the World, the background shifts from white to shaded, alerting the reader in a subtle way that Babymouse has moved into her own little dream world and outside the actual reality of the story.

TRANSLATE THE TRANSFER

Babymouse to the rescue! You can use Babymouse's pink daydreams to coach students to navigate time lines and dream sequences in traditional texts. When a few of my readers were being thrown off their comprehension by the memory scenes in *Sarah, Plain and Tall,* I remembered that they were avid Babymouse fans and suggested that they try changing the background in their mental image to a different color—the same way that the background color changes when Babymouse leaves the present time line in her stories to daydream. This seemed to help them monitor the shifts in the time line better and make them more manageable to the group. Now, I introduce Babymouse to students early in the year just for that purpose.

FIG 6.2   The shaded background in this comic, shown gray in this black-and-white reproduction, is colored pink in the Babymouse book to convey that the main character is daydreaming.

FROM SYNTHESIS TO SUMMARIZING

Most of the teachers with whom I consult consider synthesis one of the hardest comprehension strategies to understand and teach. In fact, I've consulted with teachers before who, having relegated synthesis to the end of the year, were more than a little relieved that time ran out before they had to tackle it. More than just summarizing, synthesis is the way we allow the text to affect us—not just as readers but as individuals. When reading gives us new insight, moves us on a personal level, or changes the way we think about the topic, we are synthesizing.

Recall that no comprehension strategy works alone. Instead, they all tend to swirl together in a multifaceted way that brings the meaning of the text to light, ultimately making an impact on the reader that wasn't there before. This is synthesis in a nutshell. When readers are able to negotiate among and fuse together all of the comprehension strategies they have at their disposal to make meaning of the text at hand, and adjust their thinking accordingly, they are synthesizing. The product that students construct—the actual understanding they take away from the reading—is unique to them and their way of thinking.

So, how can mere comics help us teach such a complicated concept? Simply put, reading graphica is a practice in synthesis. The reader has no other choice. Graphica draws you in and demands your full attention. True synthesis requires a deep interaction with the text on the part of the reader. Scott McCloud illustrates how graphica intentionally provokes this relationship when he explains, "Every act committed to paper by the comics artist is aided and abetted by a silent accomplice. An equal partner in crime known as the reader" (1993, 68). In this way, graphica forces direct participation from the reader, who must use all of his or her facilities to merge the comic's intricate pieces into a comprehensive whole. Consider, for instance, how the words and pictures in comics are integrated in a way that requires the reader to attend to the more important details while ignoring superfluous information to find meaning. Indeed, even the way graphica uses gutters to seal its panels together in a cumulative, puzzle-like manner—fusing their work together to create a whole entity—is redolent of synthesis in its most basic form.

SYNTHESIZING IN THE GUTTER

That said, the gutters are the veritable comprehension tide pools of comics. They teem with possibilities to practice meaning-making skills in a natural way. Once students understand the way the gutters work, they can be used as natural checkpoints from which to direct and shore up their thinking. Each gutter can be used as a placeholder, as children add to their cumulative understanding of the piece—a place where readers can predict and anticipate the next panels, make connections, clarify confusion, ask questions, make inferences, and draw conclusions.

A great way to bring this point into the instructional arena is to expand on an idea I originally encountered in Debbie Miller's *Reading with Meaning* (2002, 161). The essence of the instruction centers on coaching readers to stop at certain points throughout the text in order to reflect on their thinking thus far and to add cumulatively to their understanding of the text. Because the gutter is the perfect place to do this, students can be trained to stop between the panels for a few moments to ponder the meaning they've already acquired before moving forward in the text.

TRANSLATE THE TRANSFER

Once students are comfortable stopping in the gutter to shore up their thinking, encourage them to mirror this practice in traditional texts by pausing between the paragraphs or pages to consider their understanding before continuing.

FINDING THE MORAL

Various graphica writers present morals or themes as a central, driving device in their titles; thus, reading them can generate opportunities for synthesis. Arriving at a central theme as a reader requires a complex ability to determine important clues from the text, notice strong connections between them, and infer how those clues work together to exemplify the writer's underlying message. Take Batman, for example. If you only know him from the flippant early TV series or some of the older movies, I encourage you to take some time to get to know this character. The real Batman is actually a pretty complicated and conflicted guy. Many of the titles based on this staple DC Comics' character focus on Batman's personal inner struggle to stay within the law—even as he lives outside the law as a vigilante of justice. Batman frequently reflects on the loss of his parents at an early age due to an armed robbery gone awry. Using his anger to fuel his life as a crime-fighting detective, he often struggles with themes of good and evil, and with morals that drive questions of whether violence justifies good intentions or if a life of revenge makes up for the very sadness that drives it.

SUMMARIZATION AND GRAPHICA

In order to summarize, readers must attend to the most important concepts in the passage while—at the same time—adding them to their cumulative understanding of the text. Although it is often thought of as a short retelling of the most significant points in a piece, it's important to remember that summarization isn't just an after-reading activity. It's an ongoing process that readers update as they move forward through texts. Students should be taught that proficient readers summarize on the run while reading. Because this process is essentially an offshoot of synthesis, many of the activities we use to teach students to synthesize information link directly to the skill of summarization. The following activities using graphica suggest various ways to practice summarization with your students and make it more tangible for them:

- As readers learn to summarize, they need practice condensing the vast amount of information they encounter into a concise and manageable synopsis. For this activity, choose a short piece of graphica and, as they read the selection, have students jot down one sentence that describes the main focus of each panel. When they finish reading, they should have a list of summary statements that correlate with the selection from start to finish. Work with students first to cull the list by crossing out unimportant statements. Then have them review the leftover statements and group together the ones that are similar. Have students write an alternate summary sentence for each group of similar statements. Since these alternate sentences represent the most important parts of the story in order, work with students to use them to create a summary of the reading.

- When students finish reading a piece of graphica, have them return to the selection and summarize it by identifying one panel each from the beginning, middle, and end that best fit together to summarize the story. Depending on the length and complexity of the selection, you may want to have them isolate two to three panels from each section (beginning, middle, and end) or even one panel from each page. Students can show their thinking by recreating their selected panels together on paper, singling them out with sticky notes, or cutting them out and pasting them together (if you're using disposable materials). Have them summarize the selection by using the panels they chose as guidelines to retell the selection.

- Once you've had a chance to explore the comics panel sketch activities discussed in the next chapter, you can use them to practice summarizing on the run. This time, however, tweak it a little by having students sketch out their mental images of the most important parts of each section or chapter rather than their strongest mental images. Remember to have them practice retelling using the panels they create before moving on to the next chapter or section. When the activity is finished, they'll have a visual summary of the book from start to finish.

CONNECTIONS

This comic is very funny to me. When I laugh, sometimes I start to cry!
    MIRAKLE, fourth grader

When they read text, proficient readers consider what they already know about the topic at hand and how that prior knowledge can help them better understand the current selection. When students activate their schema to make these connections, it allows them to become more actively engaged in reading while simultaneously calling forth background knowledge that offers the necessary springboard from which comprehension can blossom.

Kids seem to make connections to graphica easily, and it isn't just because they are interested in it (though that helps quite a bit). You'll find that part of what draws kids to comics is the way graphica seems to inhabit a childlike world and way of thinking, inviting young readers into a comfortable place in the imagination—a place that's familiar. It isn't unusual for kids to show uncanny excitement while retelling a comic or to laugh uproariously during independent reading. When we encounter such strong emotion, we know a deep connection to the text has been made. Many graphica titles plug directly into a child's fantasy world, offering supernatural story lines and characters they can relate to. Return to Figure 6.2 and notice how Babymouse grumbles about her humdrum life of chores and homework. How many of our kids can connect to that? Other graphica titles focus on familiar tales from TV and movies (Nickelodeon, Cartoon Network, and Disney have all published comics), as well as traditional texts the kids may have previously read (like Nancy Drew, Goosebumps, and the Warriors series). Even the artwork in comics provides some familiarity in the way it often reflects the stylized representations our students have grown accustomed to seeing in their favorite after-school cartoon shows and movies. All of these allow students to make strong connections that support their reading.

CONNECTIONS BETWEEN SERIES

Graphica titles are often published in a series, and this tends to draw students in and keep them reading. Traditional comics were presented this way, with cliffhanger plotlines that move from one serial issue to the next, and many modern-day comics keep that format alive. Just as traditional series books hold value, connections made by reading series comics can be a valuable scaffold for many of our readers. As Regie Routman argues in *Reading Essentials*, texts presented in a series "hold great appeal. The characters, setting, format, content, and writing style repeat somewhat in each book, making succeeding books easier to understand" (2003, 65).

As students read selections from a series, they make connections from one issue to the next—often from one *title* to the next. Characters in comics tend to "visit" other characters in other titles. For instance, it isn't unusual for Batman to make a guest appearance in a Superman issue or for a member of the X-Men to show up in another Marvel title. A prime example of this occurrence is the Marvel Age series entitled Spider-Man: Team Up (Figure 6.3). In this series, Spider-Man joins various characters from other Marvel titles to fight crime. Kids enjoy this format, largely due to the novelty of seeing a familiar character pop up in a different title.

One of my students, Brandon, was reading a Spider-Man comic last winter in which Dr. Doom was the chosen bad guy. Now, Brandon was quite familiar with Dr. Doom as the arch nemesis of the Fantastic Four because he had read some of their titles before, but this was the first time he'd encountered him in a Spider-Man issue. As I reviewed his reading response log entry for that day, I could tell that he had made the connection between the two texts when he wrote, "Spiderman fights against Dr. Doom, which apparently comes from Fantastic Four."

SERIES TEXTS

For an interesting and valuable discussion regarding instructional support of books in a series, check out Karen Szymusiak and Franki Sibberson's *Beyond Leveled Books* (Stenhouse, 2001).

TRANSLATE THE TRANSFER

Recently, we've seen a rise in graphica being produced for instructional purposes. Titles are popping up everywhere that center on histories, biographies, science, and even some traditional literature. I previously mentioned using these types of related titles for paired concept reading. Here I suggest a similar idea, although now the coordinating titles aren't read consecutively. Rather, these titles are used in tandem with your regular instruction of the topic at hand. This can set students up for some great cross-connections that support your content instruction. For example, we can pair Capstone Press's graphic novel *Jackie Robinson: Baseball's Great Pioneer* with a traditional biography of Jackie Robinson and allow students' connections between the titles to support their understanding of both texts. See Appendix E, "Publishers Offering Graphica," for more titles that support content areas.

QUESTIONING WITH COMICS

Effective readers are critical thinkers who question text in a way that propels them to explore their reading at a deeper level to answer wonderings and clarify

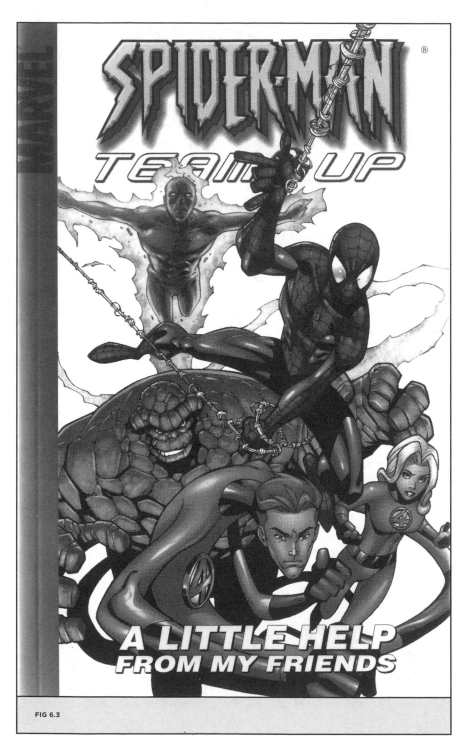

FIG 6.3

confusions. Though questioning isn't as obviously illustrated through graphica as some of the other comprehension strategies are, the nature of the graphica format still provides a lot of room for practice in this area.

Truthfully, comics can lend themselves seamlessly to any of the current activities you might do with traditional texts to support questioning instruction. But they can also offer those lessons a significant boost, because graphica has an innate way of engendering curiosity. For many young readers, the comics format is a novelty that drives them to want to know more about the characters and plotlines. The very way graphica unfolds panel by panel often peaks interest, compelling the reader even further into the story line. The busy nature of the medium requires a great deal of critical thinking on the part of the reader. Comics draw kids in; the illustrations and text foster questions that send them poring through previously read panels, searching for answers. Savvy teachers can mine the way graphica fosters inquisitiveness in readers to focus their students' attention on questioning as a comprehension skill.

Of course, as always, motivation plays a key role. Pair that motivation with the engaging nature of graphica, and you'll see why kids are driven to get answers to confusions they encounter in comics. During independent reading time one day, one of my readers stumbled upon a confusing concept in the universe of superheroes—one that has often confused me as well! It seems that there can be more than one version of some heroes in comics. For instance, several different individuals have donned the power ring that gives the Green Lantern his abilities, each one taking on the role of the Green Lantern for a period of time. Even the role of Batman's sidekick, Robin, has shifted among several individuals—for a short while, one of them was a *girl*!

All this role switching can confuse novice readers, often leading them to wonder, "Who the heck is this? What happened to the other guy? Is the original guy coming back? How come I don't know this?" It really can be quite puzzling. At any rate, last spring my student Treveon brought up a question he had after reading an issue of DC Comics' Justice League Unlimited series. His confusion centered on the existence of an older man who claimed to be the original Flash (the fastest man alive). There are, truth be told, several versions of the Flash, but the only one Treveon knew of was the youngest one. To fix this confusion, he was determined to read on and look for clues. Later, in his reading log, Treveon explained how he figured out the answer by making inferences from textual clues to confirm his prediction that there were, in fact, two Flashes: "I thought that the old man was the real Flash, and I was right, because he was the Flash before the young Flash was. He proved he was the Flash by running to the burger place." I knew exactly what he was talking about, but if you find his explanation confusing, you aren't alone. You should have heard him try to explain his processing to the class that day during sharing time. I've never seen a group of kids so perplexed! No matter, though; the bottom line is that Treveon understood it perfectly.

TRANSLATE THE TRANSFER

As with other comprehension skills, you can use the gutters to explore questioning with students. Have them practice stopping in the gutters for a moment to reflect on any confusions or questions they might have before moving on to the next panel. Once they've done this, transfer this practice to traditional text by encouraging them to pause between pages or paragraphs to reflect on any questions they have.

DETERMINING IMPORTANCE

When I shared the topic of this book with a friend recently, she gave me a hesitant look. She shook her head and emphatically declared, "Really? You know, I never could read comics. I just don't get them. They're too busy for me—I don't know where to look. There's so much going on, I can't keep up!"

In a way, my friend was right, but I think hers was more a case of not seeing the forest for the trees. There's a lot going on in graphica, and, at first glance, these intricacies can seem daunting. However, upon closer inspection, readers find that all the different attention-grabbing parts have a role in making the whole piece effective. Details in graphica aren't just thrown together willy-nilly; there's a rhyme and reason to everything. As discussed in the section on monitoring meaning, creative teams work hard to steer the reader in the right direction. Regardless, it still takes work, and when students begin to read graphica, they quickly learn that they have to weed through the various ins and outs of the medium to make meaning. This "weeding through" is a great opportunity for practice with the comprehension strategy of determining importance.

When they create comics, artistic teams don't intend to leave the reader stranded. In fact, the exact opposite is true! As students become more comfortable with the layout, they learn to attend to what's most important, searching for areas of emphasis left by the creative team that work like bread crumbs to direct the reader's processing. One of the main ways this is accomplished in comics is through the artwork. The images are depicted in such a way that they focus the reader's attention on what's most important. These intricate points are often splashed across the panel or artistically emphasized using darker lines or close-up drawings, leaving the reader no choice but to take note of them. Onomatopoeia, facial expressions, speech bubbles, narrative boxes, and even lettering are all strategically placed within the panels as if to say to the reader "Look here!" Certainly, graphica may *appear* overwhelming, but never fear: if you're a reader searching for direction, and you want it bad enough, the writers and artists will help you find it.

DETERMINING IMPORTANCE WITH NARRATIVE BOXES

Another tool creative teams use to steer readers to what's most important is the narrative box. Narrative boxes in graphica serve to move the piece along, but they also provide vital information. Probably the most recognized example of this convention is when it is used to alert readers to the fact that the panel they are reading occurs at the same time as the other panels around it, via that one significant word: "Meanwhile. . . ." However, narrative boxes aren't limited to just that. There are many ways these simple boxes can be used more deliberately to focus the reader's attention. Look at Figure 6.4—from Red Brick Learning's *Tiger Moth: The Fortune Cookies of Weevil*—and notice how narrative boxes can serve various purposes:

- To identify the location: *The Mojo Dojo. My favorite workout spot.*
- To note that a shift in time has occurred: *When suddenly . . .*
- To introduce a new and important character: *It was the Fruit Fly boys.*
- To give the main idea of the panel (or the next few panels), with the text and pictures serving as the details: *I was putting Kung Pow through his paces.*
- To clue the reader in to what the character is thinking: *The last two bugs I wanted to see during my off hours.*

When we teach students to take special note of the narrative boxes, we help them figure out what's most important in the panel. A fun way to introduce the concept of narrative boxes includes reading aloud from *The Knight and the Dragon* by one of my favorite authors, Tomie dePaola. This classic picture book mirrors

FIG 6.4 Narrative boxes provide important information to the reader.

the qualities of graphica in the way that it uses cumulative panels, gutters, and pictures to tell the story of an inexperienced knight and dragon preparing to do battle for the first time. The book is light on words, but what text is present serves to narrate the story in much the same way that a narrative box does in comics. This helps students notice the narration and fosters discussions about the powerful way narration can focus the reader's attention to important details.

TRANSLATE THE TRANSFER

Recall the analogy that panels in graphica are similar to paragraphs in traditional texts. As your students gain confidence in the way narrative boxes highlight important concepts in graphica, you can train them to use that same mentality to determine what's important in traditional texts. You might say, "Let's look at that paragraph again. A lot happens there. If this paragraph were a panel in comics, and we were going to make a narrative box for it, what might it say?" You could simply discuss the class's suggestions, or have students share them with paper and pencil. Remind them to look for ideas that narrative boxes often note, like important characters, time, location, main ideas, and summarizations. In this way, students can use narrative boxes as a template for condensing paragraphs down to their most essential ideas. In addition to using this with paragraphs, you can also create narrative boxes for chapters and different sections of text.

WEEDING THROUGH THE PANELS

Although the narrative boxes give them direction, readers still have to learn to notice what's crucial in graphica panels while discarding what's unimportant. As mentioned before, different techniques—such as the rendering and place-ment of artwork, as well as coloring and lettering—are used throughout comics to draw the reader's attention to what's most important. We can help students gain confidence in this and, at the same time, practice the comprehension skill of determining importance. One way to do this is a simple activity that utilizes those little sticky arrows your realtor uses to show you where to sign your life away. These signature flags can be found just about anywhere office supplies are sold (or, if you're cheap like me, you can cut them out of sticky notes).

As students read a panel, have them place an arrow on what they think is the most important thing happening in the panel and then bring it back to the group for discussion. Though students may choose different aspects of the panel as most critical, the power behind this activity is the conversation it stirs. For instance, I taught this lesson with a group of fifth graders using Rosen Classroom's graphic nonfiction biography of Harriet Tubman. In the story, some of the slaves that Harriet rescues begin to grow tired and frightened. They stop walking and start to talk about turning back. Harriet explains to them that no one can turn back, because, if they do, they will jeopardize the entire Underground Railroad. Then, in the next panel, she pulls out her gun and says, "Move . . . or die!" The children were especially intrigued by this panel and were eager to discuss it. I gave them each a sticky arrow and asked them to mark what they thought was the single most important thing happening in the panel.

When we came back together as a group, the conversation grew lively as the children debated their decisions. Some thought that the speech bubble in which Harriet said " . . . or die!" was critical, whereas others thought that the worried looks on the faces of the slaves she threatened were important because they reflected the uncertainty of the fugitives. Still others thought the close-up on the gun was most important. Then, one boy joined in the discussion to share his thoughts. In the panel, sort of riding the shape of Harriet's gun, was the single onomatopoeic word "K-KLICKKK!" The boy argued that this was the most important occurrence in the panel because (according to him) "it doesn't matter how much someone threatens; when they cock that gun, they mean business!" For the first few seconds, the rest of the group just sat there, silently taking this in before eventually nodding in agreement. By the end of our discussion, the children had agreed that this was the most important part because it showed that Harriet Tubman wasn't messing around. She was serious about her role and was willing to take extreme measures to protect the mission of the Underground Railroad.

Once students can do this activity with one panel and one arrow, you can expand it by having them look at an entire page of graphica and use three arrows to identify the three most important things happening on it. Figure 6.5 shows the results achieved by the fifth graders as we continued on to the next page of Harriet Tubman's biography. On this page, Harriet accidentally runs into her former master and outsmarts him by pretending to read a newspaper. During sharing time, the group discussed their process. Of course they identified the run-in between the two characters as pivotal, and they also noted the important function that Harriet's inability to read played in tricking her former master. However, take a look at the last arrow. I hadn't noticed this panel previously, but the group felt this one was crucial. Before Harriet leaves, she takes down the reward poster offering $10,000 for her capture!

TRANSLATE THE TRANSFER

Once students are comfortable using the signature flags to identify and discuss points of importance in graphica, it's an easy transition to having them do the same thing in traditional texts. You could have them use the arrows to point out the most important sentence or thought in a paragraph, or even the three most important ideas on a page of text. You could forgo the arrows and have them write down their results instead. However you choose to do it, don't forget the important conversational piece, which allows students to discuss what stands out as most important to them and what led them to choose it.

FIG 6.5 Students used sticky arrows to mark important parts on this page from *Harriet Tubman: The Life of an African-American Abolitionist* by Rob Shone and Anita Ganeri.

IN THE MIND'S EYE

MAKING MENTAL IMAGES AND INFERRING

In the best-selling book *Mama Makes Up Her Mind and Other Dangers of Southern Living*, Bailey White tells of her frustrating experiences as a young girl in first grade playing the Imagination Game. Her teacher would invite the students to close their eyes and use their imaginations to create mental images. But, White recalls, "The only problem was, I never saw anything—just black darkness. Sometimes I would peek at my classmates. There they would be, sitting on the rug with their grubby little fingers pressed against their squinched-shut eyes. I thought of the wonderful things they must be seeing . . . why couldn't I see these things? I closed my eyes again. Blackness" (1993, 183).

As I reread this passage, I'm reminded of so many of our students who have difficulty creating strong mental images as they read. Imagination is the keystone of comprehension, and an inability to visualize effectively can wreak havoc on the process of making meaning. In his book *Reading Is Seeing*, Jeffrey Wilhelm argues that "being able to create images, story worlds, and mental models while one reads is an essential element of reading comprehension . . . without visualization, students cannot comprehend, and reading cannot be said to be reading" (2004, 9). For students who struggle in this area, it's not enough to simply tell them to use their imaginations. When we teach children to create mental images, we have to *show* them what we mean. Comics can help by serving as a tangible model of the visualization that good readers create in their heads as they read. Using examples from graphica, we can mirror mental images and display them

MORE ON VISUALIZATION

For more information on the power that visualizing has to strengthen comprehension, and even a few discussions on how you might use comics to that end, look into Jeffrey Wilhelm's book *Reading Is Seeing: Learning to Visualize Scenes, Characters, Ideas, and Text Worlds to Improve Comprehension and Reflective Reading* (2004).

right there on the page in front of our students, allowing them to make a real connection with what we mean when we say "make a picture in your head." Whether you call it visualization or creating mental images, the important thing to remember is that students must learn to use their imaginations to bring texts to life.

As we discuss making mental images, you'll want to remember that visualization is more that just seeing a picture in your head. I struggled with different ways to explain this to my students until one of my fifth-grade readers helped me conceptualize it best by explaining, "It's sorta like a movie in your mind, but really more like virtual reality!" Isn't this true? The images we create while we read should change and shift with the story. True visualization isn't static. It involves incorporating any movement that's taking place; making characters' actions and expressions change; calling up tastes, smells, and tactile feelings; and including sounds—all the while adjusting these images to the twists and turns of the plot as it moves forward. What's more, true visualization allows the mood of the text to permeate the scene, though this element is often forgotten in our lessons. The comprehension strategy of creating mental images should be, in actuality, a full-on sensory experience.

So, how can graphica help with this? Recall that graphica has the ability to make the invisible visible. In this instance, it uses artwork to demonstrate the notions of visualization. Creative teams skillfully craft pictures to show sensory images such as taste and smell, and they illustrate the way things might feel using expertly textured drawings that make the reader want to reach out and touch them. Movement is often obviously noted through details in lines and shading, in the same way as characters' actions and emotions are often intricately drawn into the panel. Additionally, the mood might be expressed through different color variations, close-ups on certain characters or images, or even the overall "feel" of the frame. If that weren't enough, plentiful instances of onomatopoeia-based word art add in the soundtrack, effectively completing the multisensory experience. In Figure 7.1, the artists zoom in and out to create mood while using onomatopoeia and motion that support the text to bring to life the continuation of the fight scene mentioned in Chapter 6 (between Spider-Man and Electro). When we use comics like this—as an example of what our readers could be doing in their minds as they read—we give students a concrete scaffold upon which to practice the very important skill of visualization.

FIG 7.1 This page from Marvel Age's *Spider-Man #8* provides a multisensory experience for readers.

VISUALIZING CHARACTERS TO SUPPORT COMPREHENSION

In addition to creating general mental images, proficient readers boost their comprehension by visualizing the characters in the text. My best friend, Angela, and I are both avid readers, and we're both hooked on the Outlander series by Diana Gabaldon (for grown-ups only). We're drawn to the author's decadent mix of suspense, history, adventure, and especially the well-developed, unforget-table characters to whom we've grown quite accustomed after six books. Now, I thought that Angela and I were similar readers—until a disturbing conversation (well, it was disturbing to her) took place during a peaceful lunchtime discussion of Jamie and Claire, the main characters in the series. We were discussing our mental images from the books (we're both literacy coaches—can you tell?), and Angela just about dropped her fork when I started naming the famous actors I pictured in my mind to represent the characters. You would have thought I'd committed literacy blasphemy! It seems Angela prefers to let her imagination create an entirely new visual representation of each character she encounters, whereas I (according to her) take the easy way out by visualizing familiar actors who fit the descriptions of the characters. As she went on about the integrity of the author's vision and the essence of a writer's craft, I countered with the argu-ment that I just can't do it her way. I really can't! When I try to create images of characters, I can only see them for so long before their faces start to melt away like the Wicked Witch of the West, and I'm left with some faceless entity roaming around in my mind for the rest of the book.

In the end, we agreed to disagree, but this discussion brought to light the fact that I'm one of those readers who needs something to anchor my visualization of characters on—as do many of our students. Creating mental images isn't easy for everyone, and it can be especially difficult when you're trying to imagine several different characters while keeping them from getting mixed up in your mind. Because comics represent characters visually, they support the reader in identifying and getting to know them. As previously mentioned, this can help readers monitor who's speaking and how each character works into the story line. This visual connection to the players in the text frees readers up so they can practice attending to the characters and analyze the important role their pres-ence plays during reading. As students transition to traditional texts, they can bring this understanding with them and apply it to the passages at hand. We'll follow up with visualizing characters later in this chapter, when we discuss infer-ring character's feelings (and again when we discuss developing and monitoring fluency in Chapter 9).

TRANSLATE THE TRANSFER

If students struggle to maintain mental images of characters throughout a piece of traditional text, encourage them to use clues from the text to sketch out the character on paper, and then to use that drawing to create a comic in their minds. The act of sketching may give them a concrete, personal association with the character. You might say, "You know how, in comics, characters are drawn the exact same way in each panel and on every page? Well, try doing that in your head while you read. Every time you come across this character in your book, try to make sure your visual image of the character stays the same as the way you sketched him or her—every paragraph, every page."

VISUALIZATION PRACTICE WITH COMIC PANEL SKETCHES

Once students have been introduced to comics and have gained some experience with the way they work, you'll have the perfect launch pad for a lesson on mental images that can be used throughout the year. I developed the idea of comic panel sketches one semester, when I was having a difficult time assessing my students' mental images while they were reading. Unless they were extremely verbal or excellent descriptive writers, I struggled to get a good grasp of what my readers were imagining in their heads. This lesson is generative, in that once the basic lesson is done and students understand what you mean when you ask for a comic panel sketch, panel work can be repeated as often as needed. Before you proceed in teaching this lesson, you'll want to be sure that students have been effectively introduced to the conventions of graphica (see Chapter 4) and that they have had enough experience to be familiar with it. Additionally, be aware that this lesson should be taught as a supplement to the lessons and conversations you've already had on visualization. It will likely be unsuccessful if you've never before broached the subject of visualization with your students.

Select a chapter book with short chapters that elicit strong mental images from the reader. In the examples I use here, I chose *The Tale of Despereaux* by Kate DiCamillo (Candlewick Press, 2003), because the shorter chapters—paired with DiCamillo's excellent descriptions—lend themselves perfectly to this activity. If you have a book you'd like to use, but the chapters are too long, you can simply separate them into more manageable chunks based on the needs of your class. Working in a whole-class group, review with students the conventions of graphica (use the anchor chart created in Chapter 4's lesson) and the common components readers use to create strong mental images (movement, size, shape, sensory images, mood, setting, etc.) from your previous visualization lessons. Lead the class in a discussion of the ways the artwork and conventions of graphica support and exemplify strong mental images. Pay particular attention to the way that movement, mood, and sound are represented, and show students choice samples of graphica that illustrate your discussion points.

Create a chart labeled "Our Mental Images" along with the title of the text you've selected. Give students a copy of the comic panel sketch templates from Appendix F, or simply give them each a piece of blank paper and have them fold it into fourths, creating four blank graphica panels. (As you move past the fourth chapter in subsequent lessons, you'll need to make more panel pages available to students. For now, four panels are enough to get you started.) After you introduce the book, explain to students that they will create a panel that represents each chapter you read aloud to them. Remind them that, in order to do so, they'll need to pay close attention to the components of mental images you discussed as a class. Make it clear that you'll show them what this looks like for the first chapter, and that you'll do the second chapter (and possibly others) together, so they can get a feel for it.

As you read the first chapter, share strong directors of your own mental images by thinking out loud for students. Name the sounds you hear and the images you see that are important to your visualization. As you do so, constantly refer back to quotes or clues from the actual text that led you to visualize these things. After you've read the chapter, invite students to share their strongest mental images from the read-aloud. Dig deeply for images of setting, sounds, action, mood, and characters.

Next, model the activity by using the thinking out loud that you did earlier. Talk it through for students as they watch you sketch out your visualizations of the chapter on a half-sheet of card stock. As you explain, choose an appropriate entry for the narrative box, and try to use details, illustrations, and onomatopoeic word art that mimic the way graphica "shows" the story. Include appropriate dialogue as well, and make every effort to illustrate characters' facial expressions as best you can. Discuss each inclusion as you sketch it, and talk about why it is important to your mental image; when possible, make references to the parts of the text that led you to include it (see Figure 7.2).

Don't be shy about your artistic ability! This isn't about how well you draw. In fact, explain to students that you aren't trying to make it perfect—you are simply

FIG 7.2 In Chapter 1, Despereaux is born to a mother who considers him a disappointment—she is more concerned with her make-up than her child. Despereaux's eyes and ears are much too big, and his eyes are open, which prompts everyone to "ooh" and "ahh" at him and wonder whether he will live.

sketching it out as best you can—and that they should do the same when it's their turn. Seeing you struggle with the drawing a bit, and hearing this from you, will go a long way toward easing the tension in any apprehensive sketchers you might have and keeping the activity flowing in a timely manner during the next steps. When you are done, allow students some time to replicate your panel on their paper; then post it on the class chart, leaving room for subsequent chapter panels. Review the panel once more with the class.

You can move immediately into this next session if you like, but in the interest of actually keeping my mini-lessons mini, I prefer to save it for the following day. Begin the lesson by referring to yesterday's panel on the chart. Use it to review the first lesson and summarize the first chapter. Remind students that, this time, they will join you in the activity; help them recall the details of the task at hand. Read the second chapter just as you did the first, pausing along the way to think aloud about particular mental images, and finish again by inviting students to share their visualizations. As you begin to create a panel for the second chapter, remember that—whereas the first panel illustrated *your* strongest mental images—this panel should be a shared activity that merges your ideas and your students' various images as much as possible. Guide their thinking and sharing with questions:

- What will the setting look like in our sketch?
- What should our narrative box say?
- What sounds would you hear while this is happening?
- Who's talking, and what are they saying?
- What kind of mood did you feel? How could we sketch that?
- What would that character's face look like when he said that?
- What kind of movement should take place in our panel?

Once you agree as a class on the details of the panel, begin sketching it out just as you did with the first chapter. However, this time, invite the children to sketch along with you on their paper while you complete the panel on card stock. Remember to pause periodically so they can keep up with your drawing. You'll likely have to remind students that this is just a sketch (and define it for them). Their drawings should be quick and simplistic, not detailed mini-Monets. If you encounter students who are concerned about their abilities as an artist, encourage them as best you can. If all else fails, pair them up with a buddy—but monitor them to make sure they are actively discussing their mental images. When you are finished, post your panel on the chart and review it once more (see Figure 7.3).

FIG 7.3 In Chapter 2, while his brother tries to teach him to scurry and search for crumbs, Despereaux becomes enthralled with a sweet sound he describes as "honey."

Repeat the format of the second session for the rest of the chapters. Begin each session by reviewing and summarizing the previous chapters' panels in order. This serves as a good reminder of the activity, but it also gives you a chance to review the content of each chapter before you move forward in the story line. (By the way, this can be a great teaching tool for those students who are new to chapter books and suffer from the all-too-frequent urge to dive into the next chapter without summarizing the previous chapters or considering how they impact the book as a whole.) Continue in this manner, gradually pulling back on the amount of shared modeling you do until students fully understand the task at hand and are able to complete panels on their own. Once they reach this stage, you can move the activity to the last few minutes of your read-aloud block (and keep it there until the book is finished). The format stays the same. Each day, quickly refer to your chart to summarize the preceding chapters, read and discuss mental images from the current chapter, and then have the students sketch it out—making sure to consistently refer back to the text to verify their mental images as you go.

Initially, *you'll* sketch the panels that get posted on the class chart. However, as soon as you feel they are ready, the kids can take over this task for you. Eventually, your students will have an entire series of panels that both summarizes the

FIG 7.4 Class chart of comic panel sketches for chapters 1–4 of *The Tale of Despereaux*

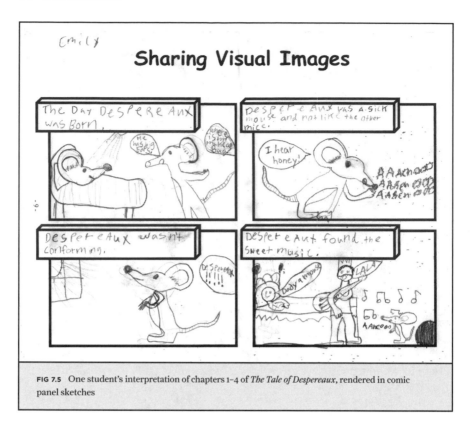

FIG 7.5 One student's interpretation of chapters 1–4 of *The Tale of Despereaux*, rendered in comic panel sketches

text nicely and anchors their strongest visualizations from the book (see Figure 7.4). What's more, your readers will have had numerous, consecutive experiences of creating mental images for themselves from traditional texts (see Figure 7.5); because of its repetitive nature, many will mentally carry this experience forward into their subsequent reading efforts.

If you'd rather keep this activity separate from your daily read-alouds, you could easily adjust this lesson by choosing a trade book and working through it page by page, instead of chapter by chapter. As I mentioned before, once you've taught this format, you can revive it anytime you think it will lend itself to your instructional needs. For instance, the panels the students produce are terrific assessment tools to check their visual images, and they also make great reading response log entries. Add "Draw a panel that shows an important mental image, and discuss it" to your anchor chart of possible response log entries, and students can start using this to share their thinking during independent reading time. If need be, students can sketch images on smaller sticky notes as they read and transfer them to their logs later on. Comic panel sketches also lend themselves naturally to activities on summarization and determining importance—I'm sure you won't have any trouble at all finding more ways you can adapt this activity.

> ***TRANSLATE THE TRANSFER***
>
> Once your students have had practice creating comic panel sketches,
> you can encourage them to create mental images using this same type of
> imagery as they read—but to do so in their minds rather than on paper.

MAKING INFERENCES

Inferential thinking comes as naturally to us humans as breathing, although—most of the time—we don't even realize we're doing it. It's the same with children. They may not have a name for it, they may not be able to verbalize for you exactly what it is they're doing, but all kids can infer. Think about it. When little Suzie comes home from school to find that the house is a mess, the washing machine is going, and her mother is standing in her work clothes, filling up the sink to wash a load of dishes, it doesn't take her long to realize that now probably isn't the best time to ask for ice cream money!

Indeed, all kids can infer. They naturally take what they already know and merge it with clues they are given to make a deduction. However, doing so while attending to the many tasks intrinsically associated with deciphering text can complicate the juggling act readers are already performing. At times, they can't find the clues they need. Other times, they don't have the background knowledge necessary to use those clues effectively. Either way, our students often need instruction from us about how to apply their innate ability to make inferences to the texts they read. Graphica, with its visual support systems, offers plenty of opportunities for practice in this area.

INFERRING IN THE GUTTER

One of the main places readers experience inferring in comics is the gutter. As students move through the gutter, they read "between the panels"—the graphica equivalent of reading between the lines. In the gutter, readers take clues from previous and subsequent panels to make inferences that fill in the missing pieces about what must have occurred in that blank space. This process is such a natural part of the routine of reading comics that kids do it without even being aware of it. Instructionally, if we can slow students down a bit and invite discussions about what they are actually doing as they cross from one panel to the next, we can take advantage of the inferential lessons to be learned in the gutter.

INFERRING FROM PICTURES

The actual pictures that appear in comics offer another way for readers to practice inferring. I encourage my students to really take the time to study the illustrations in graphica. Because the artwork is a shareholder in the comic's meaning, I honor its importance and remind students that, while it's certainly aesthetic, it's not there for pretty. The pictures have a job to do. We discuss how artists are keen to offer the reader helpful clues about what's going on in the selection. The text and the artwork share equal billing in a panel, and leaving room for graphic picture support means that a lot is left unwritten. As a result, panels will be short on text, which leaves students to rely on picture support to help them make meaning. When graphica's readers engage in the practice of interpreting the illustrations that are included with the text, they are, in fact, inferring.

INFERRING WITHOUT TEXT

There are times, however, when panels don't include text. This usually occurs in just a few panels, as an effectual technique, but sometimes entire comics are rendered completely wordless. When this happens, readers have little choice but to immerse themselves in the illustrations, searching for clues to help them infer the meaning of the piece. In *Strategies That Work*, Harvey and Goudvis (2007, 133) explore the power behind using wordless picture books to teach inferring. Teaching with wordless comics can offer the same results.

This is definitely the case with Andy Runton's Owly comics. In this delightful series, Runton forgoes any attempt at text, opting instead to let his intricate artwork tell his stories through illustrative clues presented in the setting, his characters' behaviors, and the mood he creates. As you explore Figure 7.6, an Owly selection called "Aw Nuts!" notice that—though it looks simplistic—the piece is actually quite detailed. One really has to attend to every aspect of the artwork for the story to make sense. This use of detail requires a great deal of thinking and interaction on the part of the reader, making this series a great way to introduce the idea of inferring from illustrations.

Because they are light on text, Runton's books are a terrific tool to use to approach inferential reading with visual learners, English language learners, or simply those students who are just a bit text shy. The instructional possibilities

FIG 7.6 Comics sometimes use detailed illustrations—instead of text—to tell a story.

PANCAKES FOR BREAKFAST
Tomie dePaola's delightful book
Pancakes for Breakfast is a great
anchor text to use when kicking
off a study of inferring in wordless comics. Portrayed in a very
rudimentary graphica format
with only one or two panels per
page, this simplistic, text-free,
and engaging book will generate plenty of discussion among
your students about inferring
from the pictures.

offered by wordless comics are numerous. Invite students to use clues from the pictures to create narrative boxes and speech bubbles that coordinate with each panel. Alternatively, have students use inferences from each panel to retell the story in their own words, and then use their retelling to write the story in tradi-tional format. But don't stop there! Besides using them to teach inferring, you can also cash in on these wordless comics to teach visual literacy, story development, and even oral language.

INFERRING CHARACTERS' FEELINGS

Another way graphica supports inferential skills is by visibly representing characterization. Look again at Figure 7.6. Take special note of the pivotal role the characters' facial expressions play in giving significant clues that allow the reader to infer the story line. When Scampy the chipmunk makes a discovery, the third panel zooms in on his face and compels us to notice his wide-open eyes and curious smile, which indicate his excitement. In the fifth panel, notice how his scrunched-up face and half frown function as clues that he's not happy with the nuts Owly has left for him. Without Scampy's facial expressions, this story wouldn't make much sense. In comics, the pictures are essential if readers are going to make useful inferences that bolster their comprehension. Of course, in this example there are no textual clues to support such inferences. However, in most graphica, there will be—and students can use these clues from the text, along with the illustrations and context, to learn more about inferring character's feelings.

To practice this in the classroom—and to give kids a vocabulary boost at the same time—I suggest a hands-on lesson that lets students engage in conversa-tions about using the clues in graphica to know their characters better. This lesson was originally one of necessity. I had recently consulted with a group of teachers who were concerned about a particular area on some state practice tests their kids had just taken. Most of their readers scored low on questions that asked them to identify the characters' feelings. As we looked further into ways to address this deficit, we realized that the problem was twofold. Certainly, the students needed more work with making inferences about characters. However, as we looked deeper, the larger problem seemed to be that many of the answer choices were unfamiliar to the readers. For instance, the main character in one selection was upset about losing a pet; when I put the test aside and asked stu-dents to tell me how the character felt, the number one answer I got was "sad." I agree! I'd be sad too if I lost my pet. However, the correct answer choice on the test was "gloomy." Most of the kids didn't really know what "gloomy" meant, and this was even more of a problem for the ELL readers. It turned out that, for many students, the only feeling words they understood well were the very basics: "mad," "angry," "sad," "glad," and "happy." Since the kids were drawn to comics, I decided to use them to encourage readers to study characters at a deeper level, and to explore new and different words they could use to identify feelings.

This lesson can be adapted to most reading levels, and it's especially useful for ELL students. However, for it to be most successful, your students will need to have a working knowledge of the concept of inferring and to already be reading graphica. To get started, explain to students that they'll be learning to use stronger words to express feelings. Make an anchor chart that has three columns labeled "mad," "sad," and "glad." Review these basic feelings with students, and invite them to share personal recollections of times they've felt them.

In the next part of the lesson, you will introduce the higher-level vocabulary words you want to focus on. The chart in Figure 7.7 is one I used with fourth graders, but it may not be right for you. I encourage you to add to it or take away from it so that it fits the needs of your class and your instruction. Be sure to use a level of words that is appropriate to the abilities of your students, and a total number of words that won't overwhelm them. For example, if I were doing this lesson with second graders, I would likely limit myself to three new words for each category.

Working with one category at a time, introduce the words individually and add them to the chart as you do so. In order to support stronger connections to the words, use the following guidelines as you introduce them:

FIG 7.7

1 Define the word and give a strong example of it in use.
2 Invite students to share personal connections to times they have felt or might feel that way, and clarify any misunderstandings they might have.
3 Have students identify images from Figure 7.8 that might coordinate with the intensity of the feeling.

Copyright Learning and Teaching Scotland.

FIG 7.8

This chart of facial expressions also appears in Appendix G.

4 Invite students to use body language to express how someone might look when he or she feels this way.

Once you've introduced all the words, you can continue on to the next step in the lesson or save it for the next day (depending largely on how many words you chose for each category and how well your students connected to them). Review each word again as a class, and pay special attention to any words that seemed especially foreign or confusing to your learners in the previous lesson. Review the concept of inferential thinking as well, reminding students that good readers use clues from the text and what they already know to make inferences about how the characters feel. Point out that, in comics, you can watch the characters' faces for clues, and show key examples from a few graphica titles to illustrate what you mean.

Put students into groups and have them select a piece of graphica to work with. Give them several small sticky notes and a pencil. Tell them that, as they are reading their title together, they should look for clues from the pictures and the text that show how different characters in their comics are feeling. Remind them to pay close attention to facial expressions for clues. Explain to them that, as they come across any character's emotion that exemplifies the feeling words from the anchor chart, they should write it on a sticky note and place it next to the illustration that tipped them off. Cut notches into one of the non-sticky corners of your sticky notes to create simple arrows that students can use to flag the facial expressions they notice (see example in Figure 7.9). Before groups begin to work, model this activity at least once so they can see it done. As students work in their small groups (see Figure 7.10), circle the room and confer with them about what they are finding. You might ask:

- What is the character in this panel feeling?
- What clues from the text and pictures make you say that?

FIG 7.9 Notice how the facial expressions and the text supported this group's identification of the characters' feelings in Red Brick Learning's *Robin Hood*.

FIG 7.10 Students from a monolingual class and a bilingual class explore ways to define characters' feelings.

- Does the word you chose best match what the character is really feeling? What makes you say that?
- What other feeling words did you consider before settling on this one? How did you decide?

When it is time, call students back to the whole group and have them share some of their findings and discuss the clues that led them there. If you find that some conversations need a little direction during this time, return to the previous list of questions. Revisit the anchor chart as often as needed in subsequent lessons and conferences to reiterate the importance of inferring characters feelings and using powerful words to name them.

The format of this lesson can be adjusted in different ways, depending on the needs and sophistication of your students. For instance, if the content seems too heavy for your group, you may decide to spread it out by charting "mad" one day, "sad" the next, and "glad" the day after, and then spending the fourth day searching for examples in graphica. Or you could simply reduce the number of new words you introduce for each category. If you've chosen a large amount of new words, you may decide to focus on the categories (mad, sad, and glad) one week at a time, so you can introduce one or two of the vocabulary words a day and allow the class to study them more intensely. You might also add definitions or examples to your anchor chart. You could decide to spend an extra lesson or two familiarizing students with the feeling words by having groups match the words with the appropriate sketches from Figure 7.8. Alternatively, you could have groups take the lists you've charted for each category and sort them by level of intensity, from mild emotion to high emotion. If you're working with an ELL group, you may decide that it's best to review these feelings in your students' first language before attempting a study of them in English.

TRANSLATE THE TRANSFER

As students grow accustomed to using the pictures and text clues in graphica to identify and infer characters' feelings, encourage them to transfer this learning to traditional texts. Post a copy of the facial expressions shown in Figure 7.8, and have a conversation with the class to identify the different feeling words that each illustration exemplifies. Invite students to use these sketches as models to visualize the appropriate facial expressions of the characters they read about. Remind them to base these mental images on clues from the text that help them infer what their characters are feeling. Because these are kid-friendly, easily replicated visuals, students can sketch them in their reading logs as an alternative way to discuss the feelings of characters in traditional texts.

INFERRING CHARACTER TRAITS

When you teach students to notice characters' feelings in comics, a logical next step might be to teach the use of inferring skills to explore character traits. Just as comics offer visual clues to characters' feelings, they also provide visual clues about their personalities. In graphica, we *see* visually the characters' actions (illustrations), their thoughts (thought bubbles and narrative boxes), and what they say (speech bubbles and narrative boxes). What a character says, thinks, and does can give us clues to his or her true nature. The graphic organizers in Appendix G correlate perfectly with this lesson, and you can use them to help whole groups, small groups, or individuals infer characters' traits in more depth. As students read a piece of graphica, they can use the graphic organizers to note clues they register from what the characters say (in the speech bubbles section), as well as from the characters' thoughts (in the thought bubbles section). Finally, since action is sometimes emphasized with an explosive star drawn in comics, students can list any of the characters' actions that give clues about their traits in the starred section of the organizer. Once the organizer is filled out, work with students to use the clues they identified to infer the different characters' traits.

TRANSLATE THE TRANSFER

Students don't necessarily have to be reading graphica to use the graphic organizers in Appendix G. Once they are comfortable using them with comics, encourage students to do the same with what the characters say, think, and do in traditional texts as well.

CHAPTER EIGHT

VOCABULARY, VISUALLY

Dear Log,

I learned some new words today, like *sophisticated* and *paranormal phenomenon*. Those are, like, some hard words if you ask me!

SHAINA, fourth grader

There is strong evidence to support the notion that reading is the "single most important factor in increased word knowledge" (Allen 1999, 11). In reading workshop, whether we are using graphica or not, I invite students to notice new words they encounter during their independent reading time. Shaina, one of my fourth graders, was hooked on the graphic novel versions of the popular W.I.T.C.H. chapter books. In the initial book of the series, five girlfriends come to realize that they have extraordinary powers and search for answers about their origins. As the group considers that their new powers are possibly the result of some sort of magic, the more reluctant friend, Cornelia, argues that she doesn't believe in fairy tales; she calls for a more logical explanation, stating, "I don't believe in magic or paranormal phenomena!"

During our conference together, Shaina and I discussed the meaning of the unusual term *paranormal phenomena*. We used the pictures in the panels, along with what she knew about Cornelia and the story line, to start a working definition of the phrase. I then reminded her how the word *or* can work between a word we know and a word we don't know to help us see that the two words have similar meanings, so paranormal phenomena must have something to do with magic. Using all of this information, Shaina was able to describe paranormal phenomena as "some sort of magic you don't understand."

As readers navigate through a piece of graphica, they are exposed to a great deal of new and interesting words (see Figure 8.1). In fact, some studies suggest that comics utilize more rare words than many forms of traditional text and even some forms of everyday conversation (Cunningham and Stanovich, 2001). This high frequency of new words, in and of itself, can set the stage for various opportunities for vocabulary acquisition. Teachers have begun to notice that, when students encounter words in comics that might ordinarily stump them in traditional texts, they often work at them until they understand what's going on in the text. In this way, simply by encountering vocabulary in graphica through wide reading—even vocabulary that might otherwise be difficult—students can learn many new words. I've come to see this result as a combination of two components: the student's motivational level and the visual support offered in comics.

In graphica, readers are given visual representations of specific words as they come upon them in written text. When you combine an intense motivation to make meaning with the visual support offered in every panel of graphica, the potential for new-word learning is amazing. The pictures often supply the necessary background knowledge that allows students to easily match the written form of the word with its graphic form, and an association is made. In no time at all, proficient students begin to search the pictures for assistance. As they cross-check the text against the pictures, they add this skill to what they already know about using the context of the piece to support the discovery of new-word meanings.

For those students who aren't so proficient with this method, fostering this acquisition of vocabulary isn't really as difficult as it might seem. Most readers do it without even realizing it, and it appears to happen more frequently when they read comics. As instructors, we can help this metacognitive process along by calling attention to it, making it tangible for our students, and encouraging them to attend to it more intentionally while reading.

In mini-lessons and conferences, I teach students how this process works with the goal that, eventually, they will be able to intelligently discuss their method of absorbing new words. I invite students to identify new words in their reading logs and to write about how they came to understand the meanings. I model several of these entries so students can get the feel of them, and I remind

FIG 8.1 In this example from Marvel Age's *Fantastic Four* # 7, note the frequent usage of words that are likely unfamiliar to many of our readers (*inferior*, *fragments*, *obliterated*, *traverse*, *decay*, etc.) and how the graphics and the context support an understanding of their meanings.

students that such entries should include content from the text and perhaps their own sketches—especially when they are reading graphica. Once I've sufficiently introduced this process to my students, I add "discuss new words you've learned" to our class anchor chart of possible reading response formats. Later entries in Shaina's response log showed that she attempted to replicate the same method we used with *paranormal phenomena* on other unknown words. Allowing students to choose which words they'll discuss encourages them to take responsibility for their learning and engenders ownership of the new vocabulary.

Incorporating this type of attention to new words is a simple first step toward increasing students' vocabulary. Whether it's through written reading response logs or sharing-time conversations, students enjoy discussing new words they've learned. Although their responses may be shaky at first, you'll eventually find that readers grow more proficient at this process with a little guidance and modeling from you. I was reminded how intrinsically this happens a few months ago, when I overheard a conversation that some of my third-grade girls were having. They had been reading every copy of the Babymouse series they could get their hands on. A recurring tagline in the series is that, when something goes wrong for Babymouse, she responds with a one-word summation of her feelings—"typical"—which denotes her complete acceptance of the fact that things never seem to go right for her. When this group of girls started using "typical" in a similar way in their own conversations, I knew exactly where they had learned it!

DIRECT VOCABULARY INSTRUCTION

In *Words, Words, Words: Teaching Vocabulary in Grades 4–12*, Janet Allen writes that the learners in her classroom "needed extensive reading *and* direct instruction in word-learning strategies in order to become fluent, independent readers" (1999, 11). Graphica presents a number of opportunities for explicit vocabulary instruction, and you likely won't have to do anything special to incorporate it into what you already do to teach students new words. In fact, you'll find that just about any of the traditional methods you currently employ to teach vocabulary lend themselves to vocabulary instruction using comics. Word associations, word mapping, morpheme studies, and many other lessons easily align themselves with the medium—plus, you'll have the added bonus of the picture support that is already present in the text.

SYMBOLIC REPRESENTATION

One of the best ways to explicitly teach new words is to actually *show* learners what the words mean. Again, the great synergy between graphica and vocabulary is that the pictures support the meaning. In fact, just as with the early texts we use to teach beginning readers, the act of searching the pictures for the meaning returns to the forefront in comics. This can be a great help to those students who were never fully ready to be weaned from picture support and to those proficient readers who are encountering new and unknown concepts.

Certainly, we would prefer to give our students concrete experiences with new concepts and words, but that's easier said than done. As Stephen Cary (2004, 22) reminds us, graphica can offer symbolic representations of those concepts that we can't physically show our students. I can't set Mr. Peabody's wayback machine to July 1, 1863, and take my entire class of fifth graders on a field trip to show them what the Battle of Gettysburg was like. I don't have a wayback machine. Plus, it wouldn't be safe (and it would be too expensive, I'm sure). However, as we read the graphic novel *The Battle of Gettysburg: Spilled Blood on Sacred Ground* from Rosen Classroom (see Figure 8.2), the visual representations paired with the text allow my readers to get a feel for what it must have been like during those times. As an added bonus, we pick up some interesting vocabulary words like *brigade*, *bayonet*, and *skirmish* along the way.

In their book *Classrooms That Work: They Can All Read and Write*, Cunningham and Allington (95) suggest that students participate in scavenger hunts to find symbolic or concrete representations of the vocabulary words they are studying. Teachers can modify this activity for work with graphica. Using a teacher-created list of vocabulary words that are specific to the comic they are reading, students can search the pictures for visual representations of the words. A practical next step might be to create a picture wall, which would show all of the words alongside their pictorial examples and be available as a reference for the entire class. Whether accomplished individually or in teams, this can be a terrific pre- or post-reading activity that also helps build vocabulary.

FIG 8.2 Graphica text paired with visual support can *show* students what new words mean and immerse them in unfamiliar concepts.

TRANSLATE THE TRANSFER

As students become comfortable locating graphic representations of vocabulary words in comics, consider having them create their own sketches of words they encounter in traditional texts. Through deeper conversations or even research projects, students can gain a better understanding of the words. Then they can solidify that understanding by sketching a depiction of each word in its own graphica panel. Students can base their artwork on the story line from the actual text they are reading, or they can get creative and come up with their own context in which to present the word. This imitation of the way graphica illustrates words will help solidify students' knowledge of the new words they learn, and it will create a symbolic association to them as well.

Another way to draw students' attention to graphica's symbolic representation of words is to use the following context organizer, which asks students to infer the meanings of a set of words based on clues from the dialogue, illustrations, and text. Students can then be encouraged to look up the meaning of each new word in the dictionary and check it against their determination.

For example, look at the excerpt in Figure 8.3 from Red Brick Learning's graphic novel version of Mark Twain's *The Adventures of Tom Sawyer*. The word *whitewash* will be new to many students, but the pictures in the clip, along with the text and dialogue, offer just the right amount of support for readers to infer what it means to whitewash a fence.

New Word	Clues from the DIALOGUE	Clues from the ILLUSTRATIONS	Clues from the TEXT	What I INFER it means
Dictionary Meaning:				

Appendix H includes a work page with this graphic organizer and room for up to four words. The set of focus words can be selected by the teacher or identified and chosen by the students themselves as new words they've learned while reading.

New Word	Clues from the DIALOGUE	Clues from the ILLUSTRATIONS	Clues from the TEXT	What I INFER it means
whitewash	Why, ain't painting work?	He's painting the fence in the first panel.	Tom's punishment was to spend Saturday painting the fence.	It means to paint something (probably white)

Dictionary Meaning: To paint or cover with white, for example: to whitewash the walls.

FIG 8.3 Notice the support for the new vocabulary word *whitewash*: the narrator tells us that Tom has to paint the fence, the color version shows the reader that Tom is painting the fence white, and Ben refers to *whitewashing* as painting.

IDIOMS

Graphica can be a great instructional tool for sorting out idioms in the English language. Because most graphica is written using authentic dialogue, the idioms we use in everyday speech frequently find their way into the speech bubbles of our favorite comics. Searching for and noticing idioms can build students' vocabularies and boost higher-level thinking. Studying idioms can also lend itself to language development for our English language learners.

This past year, I asked our ELL teacher Stacey Landrith to take a look at some of my comics and let me know if she thought they would be a valuable resource for her. She loved the samples I gave her, and invited me to observe as she used comics to introduce several idioms to her students. The students read *The Day My Mom Finally Snapped* from Red Brick Learning (Figure 8.4) and then were shown a chart that listed idioms from the text (Figure 8.5):

- Mom snapped
- She's a handful
- Drive me insane

FIG 8.4

FIG 8.5

- Out of your mind
- Bundle of energy
- Knock it off

After the students reread the sections with the chosen idioms, Mrs. Landrith distributed sticky notes and asked students to write on them what they thought any of the idioms meant. The students placed their sticky notes near the idioms they chose (see Figure 8.6) and then explored each idiom from the list, checking the meanings on their sticky notes against the context of the text and the picture support one more time.

Through their conversations together, the class agreed on workable meanings for all of the idioms. What's more, the kids really seemed to enjoy themselves. Mrs. Landrith later commented to me that she felt the lesson had been successful, largely due to the humor in the comic's story line and the fact that the pictures supported it so well. Of course, then she asked me for more comics.

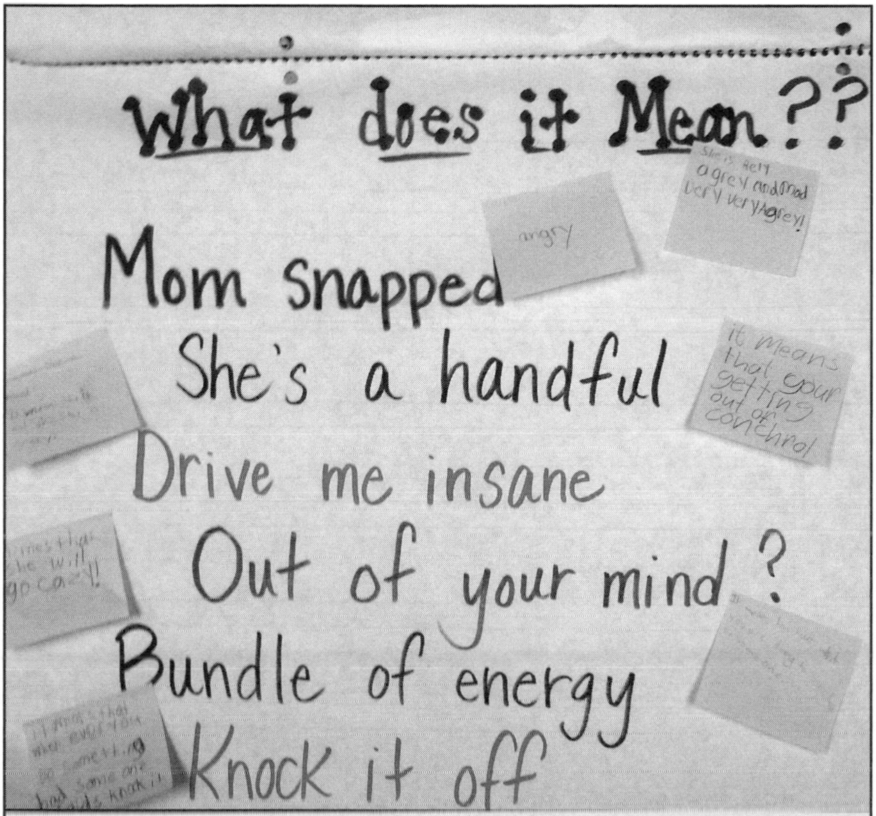
What does it Mean??
Mom snapped
She's a handful
Drive me insane
Out of your mind?
Bundle of energy
Knock it off
angry
it means that your getting out of conchrol

FIG 8.6

CHAPTER NINE

FLUENCY IN THE FUNNIES

Fluency is about more than just how many words someone can read in a minute. Though speed is certainly an important component, reading fluently is also about phrasing, intonation, prosody, and inflection. But fluency is about even more than that. Fluency, at its very core, is about comprehension. Students who pay attention to text guides and read with correct phrasing understand the text better. On the other side of the coin, when readers truly understand the text, their phrasing, voicing, and speed are adjusted accordingly. In this way, fluency plays a dual role in literacy development: it both supports and reflects comprehension. In other words, as Timothy Rasinski (2003) explains it, "Lack of fluency often results in poor comprehension" (26); however, when students read fluently, "the maximum amount of cognitive energy can be directed toward the all-important task of making sense of the text" (26).

Even without direct instruction from us, I bet that readers of comics would still show increased levels of fluency development. I have no research to back this up, but when we consider once more graphica's ability to hold the reader's attention—and pair that with its ability to motivate young readers to read more, and more often—I would argue that such a side effect is a logical deduction. Graphica's layout and style seem to offer the engaging, short texts that Max and Gayle Brand mention as natural starting points for building fluency in their book *Practical Fluency* (2006, 7). Let's look at a few ways teachers can use comics to intentionally support fluency instruction.

FLUENCY RESEARCH

For further information and research about the correlation between fluency and comprehension, check out these titles:

• *Fluency Instruction: Research-Based Best Practices* edited by Timothy Rasinksi, Camille Blachowicz, and Kristen Lems (Guilford, 2006)

• *What Research Has to Say About Fluency Instruction* edited by S. Jay Samuels and Alan E. Farstrup (International Reading Association, 2006)

• *Practical Fluency: Clasroom Perspectives, Grades K–6* by Max Brand and Gayle Brand (Stenhouse, 2006)

TEXT GUIDES

All texts offer their own supports that help the reader comprehend and read passages fluently. These *text guides* are essentially the road signs of reading. They can include punctuation, such as various ending marks and commas, along with aspects of print the writer uses to direct fluency, such as lettering style (italics or bold print) and sentence length. These signposts tell us when to pause, when to speed up, when to read more cautiously, and where we're going next. The same concept applies to reading comics. Many of graphica's text guides mirror traditional text guides and are generally embedded in speech bubbles and narrative boxes. However, once again, graphica ups the ante a bit and veers away from traditional texts by offering more obvious, visual representations of fluency in addition to the conventional road signs that students are already familiar with.

When I teach fluency using traditional texts, I invite students to examine the different text guides that writers give us to interpret the intended expression and phrasing, and I use this same method to study comics and how their text guides affect fluency. I use the tried-and-true lesson format of investigating and charting conventional text guides, along with their meanings, and then I put a spin on it by adding graphica's text guides in a follow-up lesson.

Plan to conduct this study in two sessions on two consecutive days. In the first session, bring your students to the reading area and review those traditional text guides that they already know—such as ending marks and commas as well as the use of italics and bold type for emphasis. If your students don't have a working knowledge of these, consider holding off on this lesson until you've had a chance to provide more background on text guides and how they work. Make a three-column anchor chart (Figure 9.1) that lists each text guide down the left side. Place an example of each text guide in the middle column, and invite students to work as a class to help you fill in the third column, labeled "What It Tells Us to Do." Depending on the needs of your students, you may want to bring in examples from previous texts you've read as a class to jog their memories. Once you've created your chart, review each text guide one more time to summarize.

Next, put students in groups and allow them to choose a few titles of graphica to work with. Give each group a piece of paper and have them create a T-chart. Have them label the left column "Traditional Text Guides." Direct the students to read their selections together and to identify a few examples of the text guides that are used in their comics. Have them record them in the left column of their T-chart. Once all groups have finished, have them return to the reading area

FIGURE 9.1
Text Guides Anchor Chart

Text Guide	What It Looks Like	What It Tells Us to Do
Period	.	Stop
Exclamation Point	!	Read with Excitement
Question Mark	?	Read with a question in your voice
Comma	,	Slow down
Italics	*Italics*	Read with emphasis
Bold	**Bold**	Read with emphasis or yell
All Capital Letters	CAPITALS	Read with emphasis or yell

with their charts for sharing time. Discuss the examples the groups found, and encourage a conversation about how the text guides were used to steer their fluency.

In the second session, review the anchor chart and explain to the class that comics use traditional text guides from the chart you've created together as a class, but they also use other methods—such as art and lettering. At this point, you may choose to show some examples. Using the texts from the previous session, have the groups repeat the activity; however, in this session, encourage them to look for any new or unfamiliar methods graphica writers use to direct the way their texts should be read. Ask them to chart these on the right side of their T-chart and to label it "Text Guides in Comics."

During this time, since they won't have a list on an anchor chart to refer to, circle the room and confer with the small groups to clarify your directions and possibly point out some examples to those groups who may be confused. Good conference starters might include identifying some dialogue in the text and asking the group, "How does the writer want you to read that? How do you know that's how the writer meant for you to say it?"

When groups have had ample time to explore their titles, call them to the reading area for sharing, and invite them to discuss any examples of new types of text guides they found in their comics. As groups share, use a different-colored marker to add their responses to the anchor chart beneath the traditional text guides while you lead the class in a discussion of their various purposes. Groups will likely notice examples of ellipses, dashes, and embellished onomatopoeia, along with various forms of speech bubbles and odd lettering styles. I've included an example of a continuation of the chart in Figure 9.2, but keep in mind that it isn't exhaustive. Figure 9.3 shows some of these text guides being used in a graphic novel.

FIGURE 9.2
Text Guides Anchor Chart, Continued

Text Guide	What it Looks Like	What it Tells Us to Do
Ellipses	. . .	Slow down like you're waiting for something, or fade out
Dashes	- - -	Cut your sentence short, or slow down like you are waiting for something
Onomatopoeia	SMASH	Make the sound
Broken Speech Bubble		Whisper
Tiny Speech Bubble		Use a small voice
Wiggly Speech Bubble		Use a scared voice
Jagged Speech Bubble		Yell or use a robot voice

You'll want to note that, because artists and letterers use various approaches to direct inflection and phrasing in graphica, the final list your class generates will likely not match mine exactly. That's perfectly fine, because the goal of this lesson is to use exploration and conversation to familiarize students with the various ways that writers provide clues and context to steer them toward the correct way to read.

You might also decide to vary this activity by adding a fourth column to your chart that shows an example of the guide actually being used, or by adding a column titled "Where We've Seen It" and working with the class to mark whether you've seen the text guide in traditional literature, graphica, or both.

A good alternative or follow-up lesson might include using any of the titles from Mo Willem's delightful Pigeon series as a read-aloud to start discussions about how speech bubbles are used to direct fluency. You could continue this thinking by making a chart of various examples of lettering and speech bubbles lifted from comics, or by using the examples in Appendix I. Review the differ-

DON'T FORGET THE PICTURES!

One of the text guides your students use will probably not be obvious to them; they'll use it with ease, but they may not be able to name it for you. I'm referring to the way the characters in comics are illustrated. Recall, from our discussion on inferences, how we can use the depiction of the characters' facial expressions and body language to help us deduce their feelings. That same premise helps readers to recognize how characters might actually speak a particular line, and readers can adjust their intonation and expression accordingly. Remember, the illustrations hold meaning. They're not there for pretty!

FIG 9.3 In this excerpt from Rosen Classroom's *The Bermuda Triangle: The Disappearance of Flight 19*, notice the opportunities for fluency practice as the pilots yell "TENNN-HUT!" in the first panel. Notice, as well, the way that the configuration of speech bubbles represents voices coming over the radio.

A RARE FIND

If you are like me, you recognize the value of having students read along with recorded readings to practice fluency, and you may wonder if comics are available in this format. When the thought originally entered my mind, I immediately dismissed it, figuring such a task would be far too complicated: a voice recording would totally disregard the important role of the pictures, which are the very essence of graphica. Besides, the sheer logistics of trying to dissect the pictures from the text would make it too messy for readers who need fluency practice to manage. Imagine how delighted I was, then, when I was introduced to Red Brick Learning's Red Brick Interactive CD-ROMs. These discs offer interactive recorded readings of various graphic novels from Red Brick's Graphic Library series (available at www. redbricklearning.com). The program displays the pages on the computer screen and directs the reader's attention by highlighting the panel being read (the other panels stay dimly lit) and introducing speech bubbles one at a time, in order, as the text is read aloud for the student. Specific pictorial supports are also emphasized as needed, along with a few appropriate and supportive special effects. See Appendix E, "Publishers Offering Graphica," for more information.

ent bubbles with students, and encourage them to share their interpretations of how they should be read. To reiterate the importance of meaning in this process, consistently follow up with questions like "How did you know to read it like that?" and "What text guides make you say it that way?"

TRANSLATE THE TRANSFER

Be sure to connect your discussions of graphica's text guides to the other types of reading your kiddos do daily. When they read traditional texts, students can be encouraged to imagine the way the dialogue and narration might be depicted as comics. Or, better yet, lift phrases from traditional texts (when applicable) and give students time to create speech bubbles or narrative boxes that would best "show" the phrasing and expression visually—using lettering, bubble styles and shapes, and so forth. The idea behind this activity is to let students "see" the various styles of intonation and expression. One of our fourth-grade teachers used this activity when she read a biography of Sam Houston to her students during a read-aloud during a study of Texas history. Students were allowed to illustrate the notable phrase "Remember the Alamo!" using creative lettering and speech bubbles that depicted the urgency and emotion behind this important battle cry.

TRANSLATE THE TRANSFER

Once students are able to use the graphic representations of the characters' moods to steer their fluency efforts, they can easily apply this concept to traditional texts. Encourage readers to imagine visualizations of characters' facial expressions as they might be drawn in comics, and then to read the dialogue accordingly. The act of imitating comics in this way might help some of your readers connect with the characters' discourse in a more tangible way.

Another way authors direct a reader's fluency is by distinguishing which character is speaking. When this is done well, it's so seamless that we often don't even notice it. Identifiers in traditional texts, such as "said the little girl" or "screamed the police officer," let readers know that someone new is speaking; however, in more complex texts, readers are often left to infer which character is talking. The skill of differentiating the speaker comes easily to more proficient readers, who will often change their inflection as they read to note the change in speakers, and may even go back and reread the text when they discover that they have made an incorrect inference about the identity of the speaker. However, many of our struggling readers get mired down and confused when they attempt to figure out who's speaking and when. In turn, their comprehension is halted, and the overall fluency of their reading suffers. This is rarely a cause for concern in graphica, because characters are so easily identified that even struggling readers can differentiate the speakers with relative ease.

TRANSLATE THE TRANSFER

I can't tell you how many frustrated readers I've encountered who have abandoned a chapter book because they got lost in the dialogue and couldn't find their way out. You can use comics to help some of your students who struggle in this manner. Because the dialogue is essentially attached to the character through speech bubbles, the confusion is minimized. As a result, the reader gains experience and confidence in the way dialogue works. Eventually, you can coach the reader to visualize the dialogue in traditional texts in a similar way. Students might be encouraged to create mental images of the characters' dialogue appearing in speech bubbles as they read, or you might allow them to sketch clips of dialogue from traditional texts to help make the connection between the two formats. Both of these methods can serve as a scaffold for readers to help restore their enthusiasm and increase their ability to fluently navigate dialogue in traditional texts.

READER'S THEATER

One of my students' favorite ways to practice fluency is Reader's Theater. Reader's Theater is a powerful activity to support readers' fluency development; if you've never tried it with your students, I highly recommend it. It's great for teachers, because it has the double-whammy effect of being both fun and beneficial! In her contribution to the book *Fluency Instruction: Research-Based Practices,* Lila Ubert Carrick recognizes the value of this powerful activity and cites research that reports positive effects on students' attitudes toward reading, appreciation of literature, reading rates, and word recognition abilities, in addition to gains in comprehension and fluency (2006, 211).

READER'S THEATER

For more information on
using Reader's Theater in the
classroom, spend some time
with these sources:

• Timothy Rasinski's *The Fluent
Reader: Oral Reading Strategies
for Building Word Recognition,
Fluency, and Comprehension*
(Scholastic, 2003), pages
104–115

• Richard Allington's *What
Really Matters for Struggling
Readers: Designing Research-
Based Programs* (Allyn and
Bacon, 2005), page 104

• Lila Ubert Carrick's
"Reader's Theater Across the
Curriculum," Chapter 12 of
*Fluency Instruction: Research-
Based Practices* (Guilford, 2006)

Basically, in Reader's Theater, students practice play-like scripts until they can read their lines fluently with the appropriate expression and phrasing. Costumes and props are not required, as students are encouraged to let their fluency do the work of conveying the meaning of the text to the audience (their classmates). In fact, since the goal of Reader's Theater is fluent reading, memorization of the script isn't necessary. What is necessary, however, is practice. To be able to read their scripts fluently, students have to practice—a lot. That hands-on practice time translates into repeated readings, which is the power behind the Reader's Theater. Carrick summarizes current research on the activity and writes that "support for using Reader's Theater to promote fluency and comprehension can be found in repeated readings of the text and dramatically interacting with the text" (2006, 210). These repeated readings and rehearsals have multiple and far-reaching benefits:

- Maximizing students' exposure to words
- Increasing automaticity
- Requiring higher-order thinking skills to interpret the text
- Supporting vocabulary absorption
- Increasing reading rates
- Encouraging positive attitudes toward reading
- Developing students' confidences as readers
- Expanding word recognition skills
- Increasing comprehension levels
- Strengthening fluency levels

Although scripts for Reader's Theater are commercially available, I agree with scholars like Timothy Rasinki (2003, 114) and Richard Allington (2005, 104), who find great value in adding a significant layer of learning by having students create their own scripts from the texts they are currently reading in class rather than having scripts handed to them. In choosing a section of the text to use to write a script, students develop a more intimate understanding of the text and gain extra writing practice as an added bonus. This also saves the teacher the extra step of having to locate Reader's Theater scripts.

A quick look at its layout will reveal how obviously graphica translates into Reader's Theater scripts. Compare the text from Rosen Classroom's *Chinese Myths* graphic novel with the student script in Figure 9.4, and notice how the narrator's parts can be found directly in the narrative boxes. Note, as well, that the individual players' lines are easily identifiable, thanks to the speech bubbles and graphic representations of each character. The correlation is almost sim-plistic in its nature, and students will easily take to the task of translating their comics into Reader's Theater scripts.

Before you get started, you should conduct a few shared reading activities with the format to make sure your students have experience with plays and a working knowledge of how scripts are laid out. Then show them how to adapt the texts they are reading into scripts, noting the aforementioned correlations between graphica and scripting (see Figure 9.5). Because writing a script based on comics isn't as difficult as writing one based on traditional texts, you'll probably only have to show students how to do it a few times (or less). Be sure to plan ahead so that you allow students ample time to write their scripts and rehearse them. Throughout the entire process, remind students that working with Reader's Theater is ultimately about attending to fluency—or, as my students and I have come to call it, "reading with style." Once your groups are ready, schedule your performances (see Figure 9.6) and then sit back and enjoy the show!

FIG 9.4

FIG 9.5   The author works with students to create a Reader's Theater script from a graphic novel.

FIG 9.6   Students perform their Reader's Theater.

ONO-MATA-BOOM!

Wondering what to do about all of those strategically placed instances of onomatopoeia when creating Reader's Theater scripts from graphica? Don't sweat it! They can be assigned to all of the characters, who can then make the noise in unison at the appropriate time in the show. A group of my students taught me this. When a civil war canon was supposed to be fired at a certain point in their script, they surprised the audience (and me, too, I have to admit) by shouting "BA-BOOM!" all at once. It was quite, um, startling.

FIG 9.7   Comics in which only two characters interact, as in this excerpt from *Babymouse: Heartbreaker*, can be turned into a two-person Reader's Theater script.

TWO-PERSON READER'S THEATER

Using scripts written for only two readers increases student time spent on this task and can be more manageable. Because scripts in this format aren't as commercially available as their full-cast counterparts, consider creating some of your own. The Sunday funnies offer plenty of options for this, and fans of the Babymouse series will notice that the narrator and Babymouse often interact using a unique banter that translates perfectly into a two-person Reader's Theater script (see Figure 9.7).

CHAPTER TEN

MAKING THE RIGHT CHOICES

I've grown accustomed to being cornered by teachers who like what I have to say but still have concerns that the actual topics and pictures found in graphica are inappropriate for young readers. In my experience, this is probably one of the biggest barriers to educators welcoming graphica into the classroom. Even after we've covered the issues surrounding its invalid bad reputation and reviewed the professional literature that shows its educational validity, this one worry about graphica seems to remain. And it's a big one! What makes this apprehension so problematic is the fact that, although the other concerns about graphica can be addressed with relative ease, this one has a ring of truth to it.

Have you ever walked into a comic book store? The novice visitor is often surprised by how risqué some of the displays and posters can be. Along with the expected child-friendly and colorful juvenile themes, you might see realistic depictions of violence and exaggerated representations of body image. The guys are all bulked up, and the women are . . . well . . . busty. Depending on what titles you browse, comic books written for adult readers can be quite racy; although *some* of them may be appropriate for younger readers, most were not written with children in mind.

So, are comic books appropriate for your students? Yes. And no. Many comic books are appropriate for children, but you will want to be a responsible consumer. There's no need to throw the baby out with the bathwater—there are plenty of resources out there to steer you toward graphica that is more than appropriate for your students and your classroom. All it takes is a little patience and a point in the right direction.

Ensuring appropriateness is a two-part process: 1) you need to know where to find suitable options, and 2) you need to screen what you do find for acceptability. Locating child-friendly comics today isn't nearly as difficult as it was just a decade ago, and it isn't as complicated as you might think. Some of the titles that are offered in comic shops, though not written specifically for children, are still appropriate for elementary school students, and a day spent shopping around could yield some really great results. But there's really no need to go spelunking through a comic book store trying to find suitable materials. Many of the bigger names in the industry, such as Marvel and DC Comics, currently publish comic books and trade paperbacks written with children in mind, and some of the lesser-known publishers, such as Tokyopop and Papercutz, produce graphic novels written specifically for children. Even some of the publishers you've trusted for years to provide quality guided reading and classroom library books—such as Rosen Classroom Materials, Steck-Vaughn, and Red Brick Learning—are getting into the act and offering graphica written not only with children in mind but specifically for use in the classroom. In fact, so many new titles are being produced especially for the elementary school student that it can be difficult to stay abreast of them all! As a starting point, I've listed several publishers and their contact information in Appendix E to help you in your search for kid-friendly comics.

Another way to find appropriate graphica for your class is to check out book reviews. Most of the well-known library and review publications, such as *Booklist* and *Publisher's Weekly*, regularly dedicate space to updating readers on the newest graphic novels. Many of these discuss quality and age range, as well. The Internet offers a lot of blogs and websites that review comics; my favorite by far is www.noflyingnotights.com, the brainchild of graphica advocate Robin Brenner. Finding a review publication or website that you like and trust is the easiest way to keep up with the constant influx of new arrivals (I've included more places to locate reviews in Appendix C). But take heed: just because a title is written especially for children or has been reviewed by a respected source doesn't ensure its acceptability. You'll still want to move through the second part of the process and take a closer look at the material for yourself.

When you screen graphica, examine your selections for appropriate representations of body image and violence, and diligently weed out any other questionable materials. However, don't be fooled into thinking that's all there is to it. Another part of the screening process is ensuring that the comics you offer your students to read are appropriate academically. Just because it's popular doesn't mean it's appropriate, and just because it's engaging doesn't mean it's educational. You'll want to consider themes, text level, and vocabulary, as well as picture support and layout. As with any medium, when you choose graphica for the classroom, you must be deliberate in your selection process.

If you're unsure about how to select suitable comics, or you just want a bit of reassurance that you are on the right track, consider using the suggested selection guide in Figure 10.1 (also available in Appendix B) as you preview a title to determine whether it is appropriate for your readers. I would suggest that you start out with your students in mind. Think about where they are as children and as readers. What are they ready to take on? What kind of support will they need from a piece in order for it to become a successful read? With that in mind, you can use this guide more efficiently. If you are still unsure about your selections for any reason, consult with a colleague.

I trust that you will have no problem finding graphica that is suitable for your classroom. Part of being a good literacy instructor is offering students quality reading material that fosters growth and learning but is also appropriate and intriguing. Ultimately, it's up to you. You choose what you consider acceptable for your students. You control what's allowed in your classroom. Don't settle for just anything. Be picky! Graphica is just like any other resource: there are good and bad options. Hold it to the same high standards you hold those other media, and concerns about graphica's appropriateness will evaporate.

CHECK THE ADVERTISEMENTS, TOO

Publishers of comic books often include advertisement pages from outside entities to keep their prices down. When you are screening comic books for placement in your classroom, remember to screen any of the advertisements embedded in the pages as well. Every now and then, you'll encounter a comic book that has a perfectly appropriate story line, but the pages include advertisements that could be deemed inappropriate for the classroom. If you're uncomfortable with this issue, I suggest you stick with trade paperbacks. Titles in this format allow for inclusion of comic book titles, but they are generally published without outside advertisements.

FIGURE 10.1
Selection Guide

Interest Consider the piece as a whole. Is this an area or theme that your students will find interesting enough to motivate them through any rough patches?	No	Unsure	Yes
Topic Think about the overall topic as well as the topics presented throughout the text. Are both appropriate for your students?	No	Unsure	Yes
Vocabulary As you read through the text, are the more difficult vocabulary words supported through the illustrations, context, or the content of the piece?	No	Unsure	Yes
Panels and Gutters Look at the panels and gutters. Are they set up in a way that supports your readers in tending to directionality and making meaning?	No	Unsure	Yes
Illustrations Take a look at the illustrations. Do they offer the right amount of support for your readers to understand the context?	No	Unsure	Yes
Illustrations Are all of the illustrations appropriate (consider representations of violence, body image, mature themes, etc.)?	No	Unsure	Yes
Activity Think about how "busy" the overall feel of the piece is. When you look at the panels and pages, how much is going on? Could your students continue to maintain meaning without becoming confused about where their attention should be focused?	No	Unsure	Yes
Suitability Consider your students' age level and maturity as well as other areas, such as their familiarity with the genre being presented. Is this a suitable text for the intended audience?	No	Unsure	Yes
Overall Quality Consider the overall quality of the piece. Is it well written? Are the illustrations well done? Does it look and read as if it were well thought-out as opposed to simply thrown together?	No	Unsure	Yes

CHAPTER ELEVEN

TROUBLESHOOTING

Once you begin to incorporate graphica into your literacy block, you may encounter certain difficulties that will need to be sorted out. In order to help you be proactive in anticipating these areas of difficulty, I've addressed some common areas of concern in this chapter.

My kids are "sneaking" comics while I'm trying to teach other subjects.

Don't we wish we had more problems like this? If you don't discuss this with your students ahead of time, you'll likely encounter this problem. I suggest you handle this the way you might handle any other situation you find unacceptable: put a stop to it! Celebrate your students' motivation to read, but explain the rules. Consider allowing recess time, reward time, or extra time to read comics if students desire more time to read. To carve out additional blocks of time, you might also consider holding an after-school or before-school "Comics Camp," which would allow additional time for motivated students to explore the medium.

My kids are asking to share their comics during independent reading blocks.

First of all, when students spend time reading with a peer in a paired-reading format, positive effects on motivation, engagement, and fluency abound. Certainly, I prefer that my students read independently during our independent reading block, but I think we can all benefit from a bit of flexibility, especially when our students request specific changes in our way of doing things that would motivate them to be more engaged in their reading.

In my own experience, I've noticed that, when students use comics for paired reading, the results can be quite different from what you might see when two students are involved in a more traditional paired-reading format. Traditionally, when students try to share a single text during independent reading, I've noticed that—even though I set forth my expectations that both partners focus on the text during this activity—more often than not, one partner reads while the other partner fiddles with shoelaces, stares at the ceiling, or in some way or another zones out. However, because the pictures in comics are so important to the meaning of the story, and because they are so engaging, I've noticed that, while one partner reads the text, the other partner is generally quite engaged in taking in the picture support.

I think paired reading with graphica works better than paired reading with traditional texts—it is simply more manageable. The listening partner can focus on the illustrations without crowding the reading partner, because the graphics can be seen effectively from a further distance. This isn't always the case with traditional texts, especially when the pair is trying to read a chapter book with smaller font.

Others (parents, administration, teachers, etc.) think I'm wasting valuable time using this medium.

Although it is generally less of a problem than most teachers anticipate, this issue may still come up. Obviously, these naysayers are a bit skeptical about the value and acceptability of this form of literature. Perhaps they still hold preconceived notions about the medium (see Appendix A, "The History of Graphica"). If this becomes an issue for you, one thing you will *not* want to do is ignore it. I encourage you to address this matter immediately and up front, and I suggest you do so with information. Ignorance cannot exist where information abounds. Share this book with them. Show them how the medium supports best practices. Show them the research. Invite them into your classroom, and show them what your kids are doing. Be an agent of change.

Periodical comic books are often thin, and I worry that they will be destroyed within days.

Although Superman may be stronger than steel, his comic books, quite simply, are not. Allow for some wear and tear—especially if comics are proving to be popular within your group. I admit that durability could be a real problem among some groups of students. Each group is different, and I've worked with some that seem to have no respect for our class materials, while the students across the hallway treat materials with a reverence normally reserved for the Gutenberg Bible. With particular classes, we may need to teach respect of materials. In fact, it may be a good idea to initially take the time to teach all of your groups how you expect them to handle the copies of graphica in your classroom and building.

Beyond that, there are many ways to handle this issue. You might consider using the same system you'd use with in-class magazines, which have a similar level of durability. You might allow only a certain number to circulate within your room and monitor them until you are ready to add more to the mix, once you are satisfied that your students know how to handle them appropriately.

You might also want to take a reality check. Use what I call the "eagle approach": Who's really doing this? Who's at fault? Are *all* of your students mishandling the materials, or is it just a select few? If you take a few minutes to scan the room and note student behaviors, you'll likely find that only a few students need to spend time with you to review your expectations. If this continues to be an issue, respectfully and fairly restrict students who aren't showing the appropriate reverence for the resource. Then, over time, reiterate your expectations and give appropriate second chances as needed.

To store comics, you might consider using Ziploc bags or clear presentation folders, which are available (inexpensively) at most office supply stores. Housing comics in inexpensive manila folders is also an option, but that makes them harder to browse. Additionally, many comic book stores sell sleeves with cardboard reinforcers in which to house comics for protection. These aren't that expensive—I paid about $16.00 for one hundred of them at my local comic book store—but the fit is exact. This tight fit tends to make the sleeves trickier for younger students to use effectively; if left to their own devices, some students may rip the edition to shreds while attempting to shove it into the sleeve. However, most elementary and intermediate students can be taught the correct way to use these protective sleeves if you are willing to take the time to show them. An easy instruction that makes sense to most students is "Roll the comic up like a burrito (see Figure 11.1), put it in the sleeve, and then let the burrito pop open and lay flat." Don't laugh. It works.

You might also consider procedures that would make graphica use easier to monitor, such as a separate checkout system or only allowing students to read them at the "comics table" (see Figure 11.2).

You have to decide on the appropriate level of intervention for an issue such as this; whatever you choose, you'll soon realize that most kids are willing to take extra care if they're afraid the medium will be removed from the classroom.

If you still have concerns about flimsiness, don't buy graphica with that level of resilience. There was a time when thinner, more fragile comics were pretty much the only type available to younger students. These days, however, there are so many sturdier options available that you could easily build a classroom comics collection without ever purchasing the thinner editions. As mentioned before, many trusted educational publishers currently print graphica for the elementary-age student and recognize that their products need to be more durable.

Other teachers' students want to come to my room to get comics to read.

This one's entirely up to you, but, in the end, you can't act as a secondary library for the entire school. If these students are coming to you because their own teachers aren't embracing graphica, share your success and knowledge of the medium with the other teachers, and allow them to use some of your comics while they build up their own collection. Share this problem with your librarian or media specialist, as well. School and public librarians are the fastest-growing group of professionals advocating the value of comics.

FIG 11.1   Teaching students to put comics in a protective sleeve is an easy process that can save you money and frustration.

FIG 11.2   Keeping your comics in plain sight, such as at a designated "comics table," helps ensure that they'll be handled gently.

I'll bet that your media specialist will at least consider stocking your library's shelves with some (or some more) comics, especially if it increases their traffic and circulation numbers. You might also consider advocating for a school-wide comics bin, which would house a collection of comics located in the school book room that teachers could check out as desired.

Some of my students are bringing in comics from home that I haven't previewed to ensure acceptability.

Put a stop to this. I can't say often enough how important it is that you preview the material you allow in your classroom, especially with this medium. The number of appropriate comics available to the general public pales in comparison to the number of inappropriate options out there, and this increases the possibility that the inappropriate materials will find their way into your classroom.

You'll need to decide how to handle this most effectively, but I always suggest a more proactive stance. Tell your students up front that you will not allow copies of comics in your classroom that you haven't approved. This doesn't mean students can't bring in their own comics for independent reading time; they just need to get your OK first. Set up an "awaiting approval" box where students can toss their comics, with the understanding that you will preview them when you get a moment.

One option you might consider is labeling the comics you've found acceptable (both your own and your students') with a unique, eye-catching sticker or label. This will make the comics you've approved easier to recognize with a simple glance across the room. Most kids will accept your need to have this rule and honor it without question.

My students love comics, but now they're drawing in class all the time.

Validate this type of behavior as a creative and normal reaction to the visual stimulation of comics. You'll also want to remember the value of artistic intelligence. Regardless, this is something that you simply can't allow to continue during times when students have more pressing matters at hand. So, put a stop to it, but use it to your advantage. If students want to write and illustrate comics, consider incorporating this activity into your writing workshop, content area learning activities, reading response journals, and various other educational situations. One easy way to take advantage of your students' desire to create their own comics is to offer time to do so as a reward.

I think my kids are overdoing it. I find value in using comics, but lately it's all they want to read.

My response to this concern is to ask how you would handle this with other types of reading your kids do. What would you do if a student were only reading books on tigers or poetry or jokes? You would likely continue to expect variety while honoring the student's need for choice. You would have students monitor their reading logs for how frequently they read all types of resources. If you noticed a severe inequality, you'd take steps to address it. You should do the same when the concern is based on comics.

If you do notice such an inequality, coach students to read a variety of texts and guide them into developing a reading plan to make that happen. Professional books such as *Guiding Readers and Writers, Grades 3–6* (Fountas and Pinnell 2001) and *Beyond Leveled Books: Supporting Transitional Readers in Grades 2–5* (Szymusiak and Sibberson 2001) feature organizers that students can use to monitor which resources they read most often. You can use these organizers to generate discussions with students and to encourage variety when they lean too heavily toward one type of text over others.

If all else fails, you might consider allowing students to read comics only one or two days out of the week while requiring that the rest of the week's reading time be devoted to a variety of other types of literature.

My kids need to build endurance and stamina when reading. I like comics, but sometimes I think they aren't enough.

Of course you do. That's because they *aren't* enough, and I would never suggest that they are. Again, comics should supplement—not replace—other texts and reading purposes. At the same time, remember the rule of engagement: depending on the student, an engaged and motivated reader of graphica could sustain on-task behavior for much longer than he or she could with traditional reading. You might not think comics have enough meat on them, but, if you take a closer look, you'll find that—as an anonymous source once said—"There's a lot more chicken left on that bone."

I have no clue how to level these things!

Workshop participants regularly ask me about the leveling of comics. "Do comics come already leveled? Do you have instructions about how to level them yourself? Is there a database somewhere that levels them?" One group of teachers even suggested, "You should start a web page that levels popular graphica titles!"

No. No, I shouldn't. The problem with leveling comics lies in the fact that the pictures and text are interdependent. In fact, they are so integrated that no one has—to my knowledge—come up with a system that effectively takes this relationship into account. Due to the complexity of the relationship, I doubt that anyone could. Certainly, we could lift the text from the narrative boxes and speech bubbles, and utilize some readability formula to level the words. But what about the pictures? How do we take their role into account? In traditional guided reading texts, considering picture support in the leveling process is much easier, though by no means simple. However, when you add the complexity of the layout to the words and pictures in comics, leveling becomes an extremely murky, if not downright impossible, task.

Despite this, many of the comics produced by traditional educational publishing houses offer text levels along with their titles, and you can find a small amount of professional articles out there that provide text levels for different titles as well. I suppose that, if we're using levels to help us stay in a general area of commonality, one could argue for their value. I'm sure their intentions are good—and, truthfully, I don't suggest ignoring these levels completely. They do give us more information about the text at hand and a general area in which to begin searching. However, I also don't advocate that you rely on them blindly. We have to realize that leveling texts in general isn't an exact science, and it can be even less precise when working with graphica.

All this talk about levels brings me to another point. (Excuse me while I pull out my soapbox.) I wonder sometimes if, in our little world of literacy instruction, maybe—just maybe—we're being leveled to death. Don't get me wrong. I think leveled texts, when used appropriately, can make an exceptional difference in the way we approach literacy instruction. But does *everything* have to be leveled to be useful? I think not!

I worry when a leveling system begins to dictate—rather than supplement—our teaching, with little or no regard for our students and their personalities. In *Beyond Leveled Books*, Szymusiak and Sibberson echo my thinking here by arguing, "If we know that children are unique and the reading process is complex, why would we limit our ability to match students with books by relying on a leveled list created by a company or person that doesn't know us or our children?" (2001, 15).

When levels become the "be-all and end-all" of our work with students, we've missed the boat. We mustn't let text levels limit our students, and, in the same vein, we mustn't let them limit the options we give students for reading materials.

Our students are defined by more than their text levels alone. We have to take interest and motivation into account. Think about the number of your students who can plow through a nonfiction book on whales, at a text level that might otherwise be too difficult for them, simply because they're whale crazy! It's the same with graphica. When high interest levels, uncanny motivation to read, extreme engagement, and picture support all fuse together, many students will read titles that defy the text levels we or any publisher could assign them.

I have concerns that comics are too easy and wonder if my kids should be reading something harder.

I'm regularly peppered with questions from unimpressed teachers about whether graphica could ever be challenging enough for their students. My initial response to this is to argue that comics come in such a wide variety of interest and text levels, there's got to be something out there for every reader. Many comics will, in reality, challenge our readers. Depending on the book choice, graphica can, in fact, be just as challenging as any traditional text. Saying that all graphica is too easy is comparable to saying that all magazines are light reading, and we know what a misstatement that is! As librarian Robin Brenner (2006) reminds us, "Graphic novels don't work exactly the same way that traditional novels do, but they can be as demanding, creative, intelligent, compelling and full of story as any book."

When I think about how true this is, I'm reminded of a conference I had with a fourth grader after I'd introduced graphica to his class during a mini-lesson. We were sitting on the floor visiting when I noticed that he had chosen a comic that didn't appear to be that difficult. Since we were just beginning our study of the medium, I asked him what he noticed— and what he noticed about himself as a reader—as he read it. (Keep in mind that this student was an above-average reader and very comfortable with texts that might stump most fourth graders.)

"Well," he admitted with an exhausted sigh, "one thing I'm noticing is that this takes a lot more work to read—it's taking me way longer than I figured it would." I told him that I'd noticed the same thing in my own experience, and we both chuckled about the surprising truth of his statement. Though a bit rudimentary, this student was quick to notice an irony that almost everyone comes to realize when they read graphica for the first time: although it may *look* easy, looks can be deceiving. In the case of graphica, they often are. In fact, comics are just like any other text. They come in levels that range from entirely too easy to "this hurts my brain" hard. Don't believe me? Try reading the graphic novel representation of the official 9/11 report by Sid Jacobson and Ernie Colón (2006) before you pass judgment; it's heavy reading, and it will definitely keep you on your toes!

My second reaction to the assumption that graphica isn't challenging enough is to wonder whether or not we share the same description of what it means for something to be challenging. If we are referring to constantly keeping our students immersed in harder and harder texts, I have to wonder about the value of this so-called "challenge." I mean, what are we after here? Certainly, we want our students to become more sophisticated in their ability to take on newer and more difficult texts, but we must proceed with caution. Forcing our students into higher reading levels too soon and too often can be disastrous. Kids give up. They shut down, and we lose them. When that happens, getting them back on track can be next to impossible.

I once read an article in which the teacher being interviewed said that, when her students complained that the text was too difficult, it was her cue that she had definitely chosen the right level. Really? All this time, I thought it was way more complicated than that! I laughed so hard, my office mate came running over to my desk to see what was so funny. You see, our goal isn't to throw our students to the wolves of text level. We must support them as they move toward taking on more and more difficult encounters. We need to train them to monitor where they are as readers, so that they can have a say in what's appropriate for them. We have to meet our students at the cusp of their learning and support them in just the right way so that they are challenged, but not so much so that the task of reading undermines their self-esteem as readers and causes them to shut down. It's simply a matter of matching students with the appropriate texts—texts that are just right and offer increasing levels of complexity without being overwhelming.

Effectively, what we are seeing with comics is that, largely due to the picture support and the popular appeal of the medium itself, students actively take on more challenging texts and work through them, even when the going gets tough. A third grader I conferred with described this phenomenon best by saying, "It's sometimes hard, but it feels easy." There seems to be something inherent in the motivation to read comics that exponentially affects a student's willingness to try harder texts—and succeed.

I would never suggest that comics are light reading. I think I've made my case by now that they can be just as challenging as traditional literature. However, graphica will probably be easy for some of your students. I think this is a good thing, but I agree that it can also create concerns. Critics may argue that using comics in the classroom "dumbs down" the act of reading and simplifies it too much. If you find this to be the case in your classroom, then it's high time we had a conversation about how even easy reading experiences can be good for kids.

If we were to offer only a regimen of light reading, with disregard for any challenge and rigor, we would undoubtedly leave our students with severe academic deficits (Krashen 2004, 114)—and I would never argue that we do that. However, on the other hand, we have to recognize that there can be value in light reading. I once had a conversation with a teacher who told me that, after spending two weeks on a text level, she moves her kids up—whether they are ready or not! Two weeks? That's all you get? I'm of the belief that we have to let our students stew at comfortable text levels, almost as if they are cocooning and storing up the energy they will need to soar through those more difficult text levels later on. We should allow our students to bask in texts that are easy and just right. Otherwise, it's like building a house on sand: students who are pushed to higher and more difficult levels too early will quickly tumble back down.

Allington discusses how, as adults, most of us prefer to read easy texts over hard texts, and states with conviction that "lots of high-success reading is absolutely critical to reading development and to the development of positive stances toward reading" (2005, 57). Regie Routman echoes this sentiment in her book *Reading Essentials: The Specifics You Need to Teach Reading Well*, declaring that she read mostly romance comic books as a youngster and reminding us of the fact that "light reading is essential for turning our struggling readers into competent readers . . . comic books, magazines, and picture books—all with engaging text supported by lots of illustrations—appeal because they seem more manageable" (2003, 65). We need to fortify our students' proficiencies at those lower levels; ultimately, this will better prepare them for the road ahead. Allowing our students to enjoy easy texts gives them opportunities to practice their reading skills without fear of failure. When students feel safe, they can take risks in their learning. With their supportive pictures, popular story lines, and engaging art, comics can make it *easy to learn* and offer a significant level of assistance to help our readers become even better.

I just read your book, and I'm anxious to see how my kids respond to this interesting medium.

Well, what are you waiting for? The second mouse may get the cheese, but the early bird still gets the worm! Take a look at the resources listed in the appendixes, squeeze that money turnip so you can get yourself some titles, and forge ahead. You'll find that incorporating graphica into your teaching day is a natural transition with a tremendous payoff. So, get started! There's no better time than the present.

AFTERWORD

A lot has changed since I sat down to write this book. The world of graphica for the elementary reader continues to grow, as more and more titles claim their spaces on shelves across the nation's libraries, bookstores, and classrooms. More frequent articles and discussions among scholars about the validity of using comics in the classroom are emerging, and even the weekly literature news service I subscribe to has gone from the rare mention of graphica to featuring almost one article a month. I'm on the road more than ever to present workshops about the topic, and the pile of comics that I began collecting in that comic book store so long ago has grown to more than 300 titles. I've made the move to a new school in the district, Bradley has gone on to middle school, and we've since lost contact.

But some things haven't changed. Good teaching is still good teaching. Kids are still kids, and they still deserve the very best instruction we can give them—instruction that takes into account where they are as children and readers, as well as their motivation, interest, and engagement. And we, as teachers, still hold fast to the grave responsibility we've accepted to intentionally meet the needs of every child who enters our classroom.

Last November, I made a presentation to a literacy cadre in a nearby district. It was a clear, cool, beautiful Friday, and we were all in a good mood. Somewhere along the way, we started to talk about our responsibility to share with other teachers what we know to be valuable for literacy instruction. In this frame of mind, we jokingly referred to ourselves as "literacy prophets." We had a great laugh about this, but the self-appointed title isn't far from the truth. When we find something we think really makes a difference in children's literacy levels, we tend to share it with a passion normally reserved for zealots. Comics have just begun to recover from the negative stigma they've held for years; at the same time, they are starting to take their rightful place at the table of appropriate literature for students. Perhaps Gene Yang (2003) put it best when he wrote, "I must conclude that the American educational establishment has shied away from comics for incidental, historical reasons rather than deficiencies within the medium itself."

Despite these steps in the right direction, too many teachers out there remain unconvinced of graphica's place in the world of education. This reluctance could be due to the fact that the merger of comics and education is relatively new. People are often uncomfortable with what they don't know, and it may take some of our peers time to welcome this medium into their classrooms. Scott McCloud reminds us that the comics genre is "perceived as a recent invention and suffers the curse of all new media. The curse of being judged by standards of the old" (1993, 151). I suppose this makes sense, but we must overcome this stigma. The deserving medium of graphica needs people like us to help spread the truth about the instructional value it offers.

So go forth, and tell anyone who will listen!

APPENDIX A
THE HISTORY OF GRAPHICA

Now that you're primed to start using graphica in your classroom, I want to give you some background information on its history. You might be tempted to skim past a section entitled "The History of Graphica," and any other time I would be right there with you. But hear me out on this. Graphica is continually misunderstood, and part of understanding why this is so includes a journey into the history that set those misinformed gears in motion. This section will serve as a primer on the saga of comics and open your eyes to the reasons behind those negative assumptions so that, in the future, should they ever rear their nasty little heads, you can negate them.

IN THE BEGINNING . . .

Our earliest manifestations of attempts to represent meaning through pictures can be traced as far back as our history itself. Consider prehistoric cave paintings: even before history was recorded, humans utilized pictures to tell stories.

Words and text would come much later, but the ball was rolling. Eventually, we'd see the format brought to light through pre-Columbian picture manuscripts, Egyptian tombs (see Figure A.1), French tapestries (see Figure A.2), and Japanese scrolls, and then continue through the introduction of printing and the telling of picture stories, which in due course saw words added to pictures as early as the

FIG A.1   This image from an ancient Egyptian tomb shows agricultural scenes arranged in a way that looks similar to modern comic panels.

FIG A.2   The medieval Bayeux tapestry is an example of words and pictures working together to tell a story, as they do in graphica.

mid-1800s (McCloud 1993, 10–18). The first newspaper comics were introduced around the 1890s, but the introduction of the actual comic book was still a few years away (Cart 2006).

THE EARLY 1900S: THE BIRTH OF AN ERA

Comic books evolved somewhere around the beginning of this period, and, by the mid-1900s, they were an extremely popular part of American culture. Superman, Batman, Wonder Woman, Archie, and Captain Marvel were all introduced during this time, the business of comics was booming, and readership was extremely high (Gorman 2003, 1–2; Krashen 2004, 93; Cart 2006). So many people were reading comic books, in fact, that more were sold between the 1940s and 1950s than any other decade before *or since* (Lavin 1998), leading comic enthusiasts to label this period the Golden Age of Comics.

Even more surprising is the fact that, in the early to mid-1900s, the world of education had already begun to take a strong look at the value of comics for young learners, and a great deal of positive research was pouring in. Still, others disagreed with these findings, and two sides of the fence began to emerge. One group of educators saw extreme value in graphica and even started to create curricula that could be used with it, whereas the other camp felt that comics were not in line with appropriate educational and social goals and argued for their dismissal from the realm of literature. Just for fun, can you guess which side librarians and media specialists supported? Surprisingly, most fell on the side of the fence that opposed comics—and made a loud *thump* as they did so (Yang 2003).

1954: A SHOT RANG OUT

The tide had turned by 1954, the year that essentially gave rise to the negative perceptions that still loom about graphica today. Let's take a look at how the dominoes fell. One of the major turning points came when Dr. Frederic Wertham, a psychiatrist, tilted public opinion against comics by writing a book entitled *The Seduction of the Innocent*. In this work, Wertham blamed comics for a multitude of social problems, from juvenile delinquency to illiteracy and even sexual deviance. Yes, you read that right: sexual deviance!

Wertham's assertions excited such frenzy that the Senate Subcommittee to Investigate Juvenile Delinquency was eventually formed to investigate the claims he and his colleagues made. Though these claims were later invalidated, the damage had been done, and the repercussions from Wertham's accusations were immeasurable. American opinion was so swayed against graphica that the world of academia would have nothing further to do with it (Yang 2003; Gorman 2003, 2; Krashen 2004, 93; Lavin 1998, Brenner 2006).

The party was over.

1954–1960S: TRIAGE

At this point in the saga, graphica was literally dying on the vine. Many publishers went out of business, and the industry was reeling. Though several comics publishers tried, few had the money or resources to bounce back from Wertham's vehement attack; the industry seemed unable to rally. Those who attempted to work within the new restrictions that resulted from the Senate committee did so in hypervigilant fear of poking the bear of censorship (Krashen 2004, 93). For various reasons—and despite its enormous popularity just a few short years before—no one stood up for graphica, and many felt that the proverbial nail was being driven into its coffin (Versaci 2001). Consequently, though it was largely the product of a witch hunt, the negative opinion of comics would remain in place for nearly fifty years.

1960S–1980S: WE HAVE A PULSE!

Despite having to fight back from such difficult odds, the comics industry slowly but surely began to move forward, ushering in the Silver Age of Comics. The 1960s, 1970s, and 1980s saw the introduction and development of the Fantastic Four and Spider-Man, both of which would prove to be extremely well-received, as well as the introduction of a new format, the graphic novel, which would also make strides in popularity during this time (Krashen 2004, 94; Gorman 2003, 2–3). Additionally, the world of comics started to expand its horizons by trying new marketing techniques and moving beyond the superhero comic into newer, more diverse genres and topics (Raiteri 2006). Art Spiegelman's graphic novel *Maus*, which tells the story of his parents' experiences during the Holocaust— with the Jews represented by mice and the Nazis by cats—was released during this period. This powerful and well-written graphic novel planted the seed that would, in the next decade, lead to a resurgence of interest in the educational value of graphica—but that was to follow later (Cart 2005). By the end of the 1980s, comics were once again considered acceptable within popular culture. However, aside from a small rise in consideration brought on by a few forward-thinking enthusiasts, and possibly due to the bitter taste left behind by the 1950s, the world of education remained fairly uninterested in graphica (Yang 2003).

1990S–2000: THE ROAD TO RECOVERY

The 1990s were a growing period for graphica. Originally published in the 1980s, Art Spiegelman's *Maus* earned a special Pulitzer Prize in 1992, garnering more respect for the medium from its previous critics and creating a stir among educators, who started to take a closer look at the educational promise comics held. Even media specialists and librarians—many of whom were so opposed to graphica in the 1950s—jumped on board to mine the potential educational value of comics (Cart 2005; Yang 2003; Gorman 2003, 3).

Manga also hit the scene in the 1990s, reaching out to more and more readers—specifically teens and young adults—and laying the groundwork for a following in its own right that continues in full swing to this day. Publishers and booksellers, recognizing the potential of the format, began to make manga more available as well (Krashen 2004, 96; Gorman 2003, 3). This only increased its popularity, and the demand for manga skyrocketed.

Although educators were finally starting to take a look at the educational potential comics held, their focus was predominantly geared toward higher levels of education. Aside from a few offerings, appropriate graphica written specifically for elementary-aged children remained largely unavailable (Lavin 1998). This, however, was about to change.

THE PRESENT: HEALTH, WEALTH, AND HAPPINESS

During the past decade, graphica has experienced a veritable explosion in acceptance—within popular culture as well as the world of education (Foster 2004). Keith McPherson (2006) reflects on several reasons for this growth, including an increase in the "awareness of the genre's unique strengths" as well as an increase in research, and concludes that reading graphica is actually "more cognitively demanding" than reading traditional text. Research into graphica's potential to affect young learners in a positive way continues to grow, and more and more educational institutions are starting to accept it as a worthwhile medium with a great deal to offer (Mendez 2004, Cart 2006, Yang 2003, Versaci 2001). Furthermore, a recent article in the *New York Times* claimed that comics could be the "next new literary form" (McGrath 2004), and increasing numbers of educational publishers are finally creating imprints to manufacture appropriate titles geared toward younger students (Cart 2006). Wertham's disastrous 1954 claims have long since been debunked (Krashen 2004, 94), and, although sales have yet to reach the peak they enjoyed in the 1940s, the graphic novel market has spent the extent of this decade consistently above the $200 million mark (Reid 2005)!

It's been a long road for comics, but today they're certainly poised to regain their luster of yesteryear. With manga's arrival on the scene, increased titles available for larger varieties of readers, and the introduction of webcomics and other developments of the new millennium, graphica will likely surpass its sparkle of the 1940s. Surely, all's well that ends well; as Steve Raiteri states in an article for *Library Journal,* "There has never been a better time than the present to be a comics fan" (2006, 86).

The Evolution of Comics	Date	Education's View of Graphica
	1800	
Picture stories introduced	1850	
Newspaper comics introduced	1900	
Comic books introduced		
		Research into educational value of comics begins
Superman and other popular characters introduced, kicking off the Golden Age of Comics		Two sides of the debate form
	1950	
Seduction of the Innocent published; Senate Review Committee formed; Bad reputation begins	1960	Investigation of comics' educational value comes to a standstill
Silver Age of Comics begins as new popular characters are introduced and familiar ones are brought back	1970	
		Slight increase in educational interest in comics
Graphic novel introduced with Will Eisner's *A Contract with God*	1980	
Art Spiegelman's *Maus* published		
	1990	Academia begins to see that graphica can be mined for a multitude of educational purposes
Maus wins Pulitzer		
Manga gains in popularity in the United States	2000	National Association of Comics Art Educators founded (2001)
Publishers start to produce comics specifically created for younger, elementary-aged readers		Maryland State Department of Education begins Comic Book Initiative (2005)
		Comics gain greater respectability and visibility in educational journals, research, and lessons

APPENDIX B

SELECTION GUIDE

Interest Consider the piece as a whole. Is this an area or theme that your students will find interesting enough to motivate them through any rough patches?	No	Unsure	Yes
Topic Think about the overall topic as well as the topics presented throughout the text. Are both appropriate for your students?	No	Unsure	Yes
Vocabulary As you read through the text, are the more difficult vocabulary words supported through the illustrations, context, or the content of the piece?	No	Unsure	Yes
Panels and Gutters Look at the panels and gutters. Are they set up in a way that supports your readers in tending to directionality and making meaning?	No	Unsure	Yes
Illustrations Take a look at the illustrations. Do they offer the right amount of support for your readers to understand the context?	No	Unsure	Yes
Illustrations Are all of the illustrations appropriate (consider representations of violence, body image, mature themes, etc.)?	No	Unsure	Yes
Activity Think about how "busy" the overall feel of the piece is. When you look at the panels and pages, how much is going on? Could your students continue to maintain meaning without becoming confused about where their attention should be focused?	No	Unsure	Yes
Suitability Consider your students' age level and maturity as well as other areas, such as their familiarity with the genre being presented. Is this a suitable text for the intended audience?	No	Unsure	Yes
Overall Quality Consider the overall quality of the piece. Is it well written? Are the illustrations well done? Does it look and read as if it were well thought-out as opposed to simply thrown together?	No	Unsure	Yes

APPENDIX C
WEBSITES

The Internet is loaded with resources for learning more about graphica and using it in the classroom. However, sometimes doing a search on the Web can be like opening Pandora's Box! Some of what you'll find is useful, and some is . . . not so much. To help you with this issue, I've listed some resources that I think you'll find valuable as you continue your journey into the world of graphica. For simplicity, I've sorted them according to each website's primary focus.

In the "Activities" section, you'll find activities and lessons that you can use with your students. Under "Reviews," you'll find websites and blogs from people and institutions that review graphica on a regular basis. Please know that, although I'm listing these here for your reference, I haven't read every book these sites review and therefore can't vouch for each listing. Review sites are just a starting point. Regardless of who suggests a particular title, I encourage you to be a responsible consumer and screen it yourself before using it instructionally. In the final section, entitled "More Information," I've listed websites that can direct you to additional information about the medium.

ACTIVITIES

www.comics.com

This site publishes newspaper "funnies" of all types and allows you to search for them by the date they were published. You can also get more information about the popular Shortcuts educational pages included in many national papers, along with teaching guides that coordinate with them.

http://www.scholastic.com/goosebumpsgraphix/makeyourown/index.htm

This is a fun site that features a comic creator kids can use to make their own versions of the popular Goosebumps graphic novels. The comic creator is set up so that users can choose the characters, setting, and speech bubbles, as well as add their own text. It's quite user friendly, and students can print out their comic when they're done. This is a great writing connection!

http://www.scholastic.com/captainunderpants/comic.htm

This is a fun site for fans of Captain Underpants. It's similar to the Goosebumps comic creator, but this one is limited in that users have to choose the text and dialogue from a set of options rather than create their own.

http://www.makebeliefscomix.com/

This fun comic creator features original, kid-friendly characters. It's also easy to use, and it offers a wide range of options for kids to choose from. It's a terrific writing activity that would make a great workstation!

www.professorgarfield.com

This is a site based on the popular comic strip character Garfield. Kids can go to the "Comics Lab" to create their own Garfield comic strip, and teachers can find ways to use the site educationally by visiting the "Teacher's Lounge."

www.marvelkids.com

In this interactive website, students can explore the Marvel world with games, videos, and additional information. They can also get to know the characters better and even read some of the digital comics made available free of charge.

www.readwritethink.org

This is an excellent site for literacy-based lesson plans that was created through a partnership between the International Reading Association and the National Council of Teachers of English. Search for "comics," and the search engine will return more than ten lessons that use comics in the classroom.

http://www.readwritethink.org/materials/comic/index.html

This is a comic creator from ReadWriteThink. It's a bit more difficult to use than some of the other comic creators listed here, but it's still kid friendly.

www.comiclife.com

This is a link to the main page of an excellent program that you can use to create personalized graphica with your own digital photos. It's simple to use, relatively inexpensive, and the website offers a no-cost, thirty-day trial if you want to try it before you buy it. Imagine using photos of your students to create meaningful and engaging comics—or, better yet, letting your students do it themselves! Keep in mind that, because your final products will be laden with word art and digital photos, they may take up more memory than a typical document. If that's an issue for you, consider using a memory stick to store your students' creations.

REVIEWS

www.noflyingnotights.com

This excellent site, which features reviews of graphica for youth, teens, and adults, is maintained by librarian Robin Brenner. Go to the "Sidekicks" page for elementary titles.

www.graphicclassroom.blogspot.com

This blog was established to help teachers and librarians gain a better understanding of graphica's possibilities by helping them locate "high qual- ity, educational-worthy graphic novels and comics." Each review includes a synopsis, a review of the text and art, a rating of its appropriateness for the classroom, and suggestions about how the title might be used academically. The reviewer also includes areas to be aware of (for example, language, art, themes, and violence), which is really helpful. You can even submit titles for review.

www.amazon.com

Amazon.com keeps a terrific stock of great graphica titles for children; once you start your search, you'll be directed to even more possibilities and lists. A little searching on your part can turn up a gold mine of possibilities, like the Artemis Fowl (Hyperion) and Redwall (Philomel) graphic novels, which I found on Amazon.com well before any other site tipped me off to them!

www.comicsintheclassroom.net

This website, run by Scott Tingley, an early-elementary grades teacher, provides a lot of good information about comics in the classroom; it includes review lists, recommendations, and author interviews. Check out his "Big All-Ages List," which features title reviews and age-appropriate ranges as well as justifications for those age ranges. The site also lists several great all-ages webcomics and some lesson plans.

www.kidslovecomics.com

This great site is maintained by Kids Love Comics, a nonprofit organization comprising various members from all sides of the comics and educational branches, whose goal is to support parent and educator awareness of appropriate titles and their value. The webmasters regularly review new titles that get their "seal of approval" and offer links for more information.

www.allagesreads.blogspot.com

This is another review site that categorizes selections by their appropriateness for children, along with justifications for those decisions. This site is unique in that two elementary-aged students—along with a teacher (and mother)—help with the reviews.

http://www.ala.org/ala/booklinksbucket/graphicnovelsforyounger.htm

This is a link to an American Library Association article written by Michele Gorman, the author of *Getting Graphic! Using Graphic Novels to Promote Literacy with Preteens and Teens* (2003), in which she lists and discusses thirty graphica titles that she recommends for elementary readers.

• • •

You'll also find that several traditional review sources examine children's graphica on a regular basis. For example, *Library Media Connection* recently began a regular review of graphica called "Getting Graphic," which is written by Allyson Lyga, author of *Graphic Novels in Your Media Center: A Definitive Guide* (2004). Many of these review publications are names you've trusted to give you solid information for years!

Booklist (www.ala.org/booklist)
The Comics Journal (www.tcj.com)
Publisher's Weekly (www.publishersweekly.com)
Library Journal (www.libraryjournal.com)
School Library Journal (www.slj.com)
Library Media Connection (www.linworth.com/lmc)

MORE INFORMATION

www.comicshoplocator.com

This site links to a locator service that helps you find comic book stores in your area. All you have to do is enter your zip code, and the locator will tell you how to find the store nearest to your home. The same information is available via the locator's toll-free number: 1-888-266-4226.

www.teachingcomics.org

This is the website for the National Association of Comics Art Educators (NACAE). On the bottom of the main page, click on "Links" to find online articles, research, information, additional websites, and activities for using comics academically.

www.andyrunton.com

This is the website of Owly creator Andy Runton. Click on "Comics" near the top of the page to see several samples of his work.

www.freecomicbookday.com

An event usually held on the first Saturday in May, Free Comic Book Day is a movement with the goal of introducing graphica to people who are unfamiliar with the medium. Go to the site for more information on participating comics shops and how to get a free comic book!

www.coverconcepts.com

Cover Concepts is a division of Marvel Comics that offers free materials to schools.

www.babymouse.com

This is the home page of Random House's popular Babymouse series by Jennifer and Matthew Holm. Rendered in black, white, and pink, the writers of Babymouse offer a series of graphic novels that share the happenings of a very imaginative young mouse who's just trying to make it from one day to the next. Girls are drawn to this text because the main character's struggles are so true to life. Whether the problem is getting invited to a popular student's sleepover, dealing with a sunburn, or deciding where to sit on the bus—if Babymouse is stressing over it, chances are your young female readers have as well.

APPENDIX D

SUGGESTED TITLES

Once teachers become interested in using graphica to teach comprehension and motivate readers, the next logical question becomes: Where can I find some good titles? In addition to information from the websites in Appendix C and the publishers discussed in Appendix E, you'll find several different lists in this appendix that will help you move forward in your search for graphica-based resources. We start out with a top ten list of favorite titles submitted by Robin Brenner, and then move into graphica-style picture books, comics that appeal to female readers, and wordless comics. Then, we'll finish up with a collection of bridge comics titles. As always, I encourage you to refer to the selection guide in Appendix B as you review these titles. Whereas some titles are highly appropriate for certain groups of students, they might be just as inappropriate for others.

ROBIN BRENNER'S TOP TEN ELEMENTARY SCHOOL GRAPHIC NOVELS

Robin is a teen librarian at the Brookline Public Library in Brookline, Massachusetts, and creator and editor-in-chief of the website www.noflyingnotights. com. At my request, she has graciously contributed this list of her favorites in the field, and you'll notice that some of her suggestions overlap with my own recommendations.

Yotsuba&! series
by Kiyohiko Azuma
ADV Manga, 2005–present
Yotsuba is an incredibly naive little girl (or maybe she's an alien?), but she's also cute without being insipid. You can marvel with her at the wonder of doorbells and the brilliance of fireworks, and stand in awe of great pastries. This series, a slice-of-life story with a charming, hilarious character at its core, finds humor in everyday matters, and Azuma is the master of the well-timed punch line.

Akiko series
by Mark Crilley
Sirius Entertainment, 2003–present
The Menace of Alia Rellapor (Volumes 1–3)
As a fourth grader looking for adventure, Akiko knows that friendship, loyalty, daring, smarts, and tenacity will get you everywhere, even if you've been transported to another world. These graphic novels include companion prose novels that continue their stories, and Mark Crilley's charm and imagination shine in both versions.

Babymouse series
by Jennifer Holm and Matthew Holm
Random House Books for Young Readers, 2005–present
Babymouse: Queen of the World; Babymouse: Our Hero; Babymouse: Beach Babe; Babymouse: Rock Star; Babymouse: Heartbreaker; Babymouse: Camp Babymouse; Babymouse: Skater Girl; Babymouse: Puppy Love
She's spunky, she's pink, she's outspoken—she's Babymouse! She's trying to figure it all out: popularity, friendship, fame, and just which rockin' career she wants to tackle next. She dreams of fantastic worlds before facing her fear of dodgeball and trying to get invited to the party of the year, but in the end Babymouse is all about how to make it through her time right here on planet Earth.

Clan Apis
by Jay Hosler
Active Synapse, 2000
Nyuki is a newborn bee, but she's not ready to do as she's told. Why does

she have to leave her cozy home as a larva? How can she figure out where to find the best pollen? What are all of her brothers and sisters up to, anyway? With a bee's-eye view of the world, this book explores every part of a bee's life with wit and pathos. Best of all, it's packed full of great information without feeling like a textbook.

Magic Pickle series
by Scott Morse
Graphix, 2008
Magic Pickle and The Planet of the Grapes; Magic Pickle vs. The Egg Poacher
He fights for justice, truth, and good vegetables everywhere! Meet Magic Pickle, a superhero who, despite being a giant kosher pickle brought to life, is as stoic, brave, and righteous as any of those other guys with capes. With the help of his human friend Jojo, a spunky eight-year-old, he aims to defeat the Brotherhood of Evil Produce once and for all.

Mouse Guard: Fall 1152
by David Peterson
Archaia, 2007
Three mice sent to patrol their settlement's borders uncover a resurrected legend and a growing threat to their community's hard-won peace and safety. With rich painting and a keen sense of dramatic pacing, this volume begins what promises to be a compelling epic akin to Brian Jacques's Redwall series.

To Dance: A Ballerina's Graphic Novel
by Siena Cherson Siegel and Mark Siegel
Atheneum/Richard Jackson Books, 2006
Growing up in the world of professional ballet means a lot of things: working hard, balancing school and studio, eating less, fearing injury, and battling stage fright. In the end, though, it all comes down to one thing—the joy you feel when you dance, and dance well. This volume beautifully captures the exuberance and toil involved in becoming a ballerina at the New York City Ballet during Balanchine's leadership.

Bone series
by Jeff Smith

Graphix, 2005–present
Out of Boneville (Volume 1); *The Great Cow Race* (Volume 2); *Eyes of the Storm* (Volume 3); *Dragonslayer* (Volume 4); *Rock Jaw Master of the Eastern Border* (Volume 5); *Old Man's Cave* (Volume 6); *Ghost Circles* (Volume 7)
(The individual titles are available in both color and black and white. The complete series is available in one volume—black and white—through Cartoon Books, 2004.)
When the three Bone cousins get kicked out of Boneville, they never expect to end up on an epic adventure involving destiny, cows, betrayal, and a whole lot of sinister, bumbling rat creatures that want to bake them into quiches. This incredibly popular series is one of those tales that appeals to the widest range of kids, teens, and adults, making it a great story to share.

Owly Series
by Andy Runton
Top Shelf Productions
The Way Home and The Bittersweet Summer (Volume 1); *Just a Little Blue* (Volume 2); *Flying Lessons* (Volume 3); *A Time to Be Brave* (Volume 4)
Told using characters who speak in pictograms rather than words, this series follows the adventures of a small owl named Owly and his friends. The themes of friendship, loneliness, prejudice, and adventure are touched on in sweet and simple chapters, and the small format makes it especially appealing for smaller hands.

Amelia Rules! series
by Jimmy Gownley
Renaissance Press
The Whole World's Crazy (Volume 1); *What Makes You Happy* (Volume 2); *Superheroes* (Volume 3); *When the Past is a Present* (Volume 4)
Ten-year-old Amelia McBride is a kid you feel like you know: she's smart, funny, flummoxed by stupid boy behavior (but enjoys the teasing it allows), and still a bit fragile from her parents' divorce (not that she'd let you see that). She braves a new neighborhood, new friends, and rebuilding her life with her mom and older sister. Gownley's art is strongly influenced by Charles Schulz's Peanuts but is also very much his own, and Amelia is a heroine for all ages.

• • •

Also be on the lookout for excellent upcoming titles, including the new Flight Explorer anthology and *Amulet* by Kazu Kibuishi.

PICTURE BOOKS IN GRAPHICA FORMAT

Once you start looking, you'll find that several graphica options are available in traditional picture book format. These books are similar to the picture books we all enjoy, but they're written either partially or fully using the conventions of graphica. Because of this, several of these titles would easily fall into the bridge comics category as well. These books are easy to see during a whole-group lesson, and this makes them terrific tools with which to introduce the graphica format. Here's a list of a few titles to get you started.

The Knight and the Dragon by Tomie dePaola (Putnam Juvenile, 1998)

The Legend of Hong Kil Dong: The Robin Hood of Korea by Anne Sibley O'Brien (Charlesbridge, 2006)

The Day I Swapped My Dad for Two Goldfish by Neil Gaiman (Bloomsbury, 2004)

Who's Got Game? Poppy or the Snake? by Toni and Slade Morrison (Scribner, 2003)

Who's Got Game? The Lion or the Mouse? by Toni and Slade Morrison (Scribner, 2003)

Shark and Lobster's Amazing Undersea Adventure by Viviane Schwarz (Candlewick, 2006)

The Clouds Above by Jordan Crane (Fantagraphics Books, 2005)

Jackie and the Shadow Snatcher by Larry Di Fiori (Knopf Books for Young Readers, 2006)

The Park Bench by Fumiko Takeshita (Kane/Miller, 1989)

Don't Let the Pigeon Drive the Bus! by Mo Willems (Hyperion, 2003)

The Pigeon Finds a Hot Dog! by Mo Willems (Hyperion, 2004)

Don't Let the Pigeon Stay Up Late! by Mo Willems (Hyperion, 2006)

Knuffle Bunny: A Cautionary Tale by Mo Willems (Hyperion, 2004)

Today I Will Fly! by Mo Willems (Hyperion, 2007)

Today I Am Invited to a Party! By Mo Willems (Hyperion, 2007)

Mrs. Watson Wants Your Teeth by Allison McGhee (Scholastic, 2007)

Mouse Mess by Linnea Riley (Scholastic, 1997)

Over the Moon by Rachel Vail (Scholastic, 1998)

The Burglar's Breakfast by Felicity Everett (Usborne Books, 2003)

Cuddly Dudley by Jez Alborough (Candlewick, 1995)

Seadogs: An Epic Ocean Operetta by Lisa Wheeler (Aladdin, 2006)

COMICS THAT APPEAL TO GIRLS

Although graphica was traditionally written for male audiences, we're starting to see more and more titles that speak to female readers. If you're looking to start a collection of comics geared toward girls' interests, give these titles a try.

Babymouse #1: Queen of the World (first in a series) by Jennifer Holm and Matthew Holm (Random House, 2005)

Fashion Kitty by Charise Mericle Harper (Hyperion, 2005)

Peach Fuzz, Vol. 1 (first in a series) by Lindsay Cibos and Jared Hodges (Tokyopop, 2005)

Nancy Drew Graphic Novels: *Girl Detective #1—The Demon of River Heights* (first in a series) by Stefan Petrucha and Sho Murase (Papercutz, 2005)

Totally Spies Graphic Novels: *Totally Spies #1 The O.P* (first in a series) by Marthon Team (Papercutz, 2006)

Kim Possible Cine-Manga, Vol. 1 (first in a series) by Bob Schooley and Mark McCorkle (Tokyopop, 2003)

Atomic Comics (Atomic Betty)—Galactic Issue #1: *Cosmic Cake* (first in a series) by Action Figueroa (Grosset and Dunlap, 2005)

The Baby-Sitters Club: *Kristy's Great Idea* (first in a series) by Ann Martin (Graphix, 2006)

To Dance: A Ballerina's Graphic Novel by Siena Cherson Siegel and Mark Siegel (Aladdin Paperbacks, 2006)

W.I.T.C.H. Graphic Novel: *The Power of Friendship—Book #1* (first in a series) by TK (Volo, 2005)

WORDLESS COMICS

Graphica that doesn't include words has great instructional value—specifically for discussions about visualization and inferring. They're also a great way to introduce the importance pictures play in making meaning in graphica. If you enjoyed the Owly excerpt in Chapter 7 and want to explore more resources like it, you may find the following titles of interest.

Tuesday by David Wiesner (Clarion Books, 1991)

Flotsam by David Wiesner (Clarion Books, 2006)

Owly: Volume 1, *The Way Home and The Bittersweet Summer* by Andy Runton (Top Shelf Productions, 2004)

Owly: Volume 2, *Just a Little Blue* by Andy Runton (Top Shelf Productions, 2005)

Owly: Volume 3, *Flying Lessons* by Andy Runton (Top Shelf Productions, 2005)

Owly: Volume 4, *A Time to Be Brave* by Andy Runton (Top Shelf Productions, 2007)

Li'l Santa by Thierry Robin and Lewis Trondheim (Nantier Beall Minoustchine, 2002)

Happy Halloween, Li'l Santa by Thierry Robin and Lewis Trondheim (Nantier Beall Minoustchine, 2003)

Pancakes for Breakfast by Tomie dePaola (Voyager Books, 1978)

The Snowman by Raymond Briggs (Random House, 1978)

BRIDGE COMICS

In Chapter 5 I discussed the way bridge comics can help readers transition from graphica to traditional texts. Teachers looking for more titles in this format will find the starter list below valuable.

Diary of a Wimpy Kid (Amulet Books)
This comic follows a hilarious school year in the life of Greg Heffly, an undersized weakling, who's just trying to make it through the day.

Abadazad series (Disney Enterprises)

> In this series of bridge comics, a tough-talking, wisecracking teen enters the Oz-like world of Abadazad to rescue her missing brother from the Lanky Man.

The Black Belt Club series (Scholastic)

> This series follows a group of four specially chosen karate students who learn the value of friendship and teamwork while fighting the forces of evil.

The Magic School Bus series (Scholastic)

> Most of us are familiar with this popular series about students who take magical field trips in their enchanted school bus. Both the original titles and the newer Magic School Bus chapter books are great examples of texts that merge comics with traditional texts.

Supertwins series (Scholastic Reader)

> You might remember the Scholastic Reader imprint by its former name, Hello Readers. In this enjoyable beginning chapter book series, Timmy and Tabby are superheroes who face the same problems normal kids do. With titles like *Supertwins Meet the Bad Dogs from Space* and *Supertwins and the Tooth Trouble*, your young readers are sure to connect with this series.

The Invention of Hugo Cabret (Scholastic)

> Although it doesn't exactly use conventions of graphica, this excellent tale mixes 284 original drawings with traditional text to tell its story in a way that is reminiscent of the format of bridge comics.

Red Brick Learning's Graphic Flash series (www.redbricklearning.com)

> This kid-friendly series offers four different historical fiction titles in bridge comic format:
>
> > *Blackbeard's Sword: The Pirate King of the Carolinas*
> > *Fire and Snow: A Tale of the Alaskan Gold Rush*
> > *Hot Iron: The Adventures of a Civil War Powder Boy*
> > *The Last Rider: The Final Days of the Pony Express*

APPENDIX E

PUBLISHERS OFFERING GRAPHICA

The collection of available children's graphica is currently in the midst of a massive growth spurt. Additional titles are introduced almost weekly, and staying well versed on all of them can be downright exhausting—if not impossible. You could easily spend days researching and poring through all of the current titles. However, the problem would be that, by the time you'd completed your task, several more titles would have been introduced. With that in mind, I've listed a few publishers, along with their contact information, to help direct your search. To assist you further, I've sorted the list into two groups: general publishers (those who publish titles for the general public) and educational publishers (those who publish titles mainly for classroom and educational use).

GENERAL PUBLISHERS

MARVEL

Marvel is what comic enthusiasts refer to as one of the "top two" publishers, and it is well known for its popular characters like Spider-Man, the Fantastic Four, and the X-Men. Marvel offers titles that are advertised as appropriate for all ages under their Marvel Adventures imprint. This imprint was originally called Marvel Age, but it became Marvel Adventures in 2005. Among kid-friendly versions of X-Men,

Spider-Man, the Fantastic Four, the Hulk, the Avengers, and more, your readers are sure to find a title that will interest them. Kid superheroes like Power Pack, Gus Beezer, and Franklin Richard: Son of a Genius will especially appeal to younger readers.

Marvel's website is built to offer more than a list of titles. It's a good place to get familiar with the characters and series that are available. You'll want to search carefully within the Marvel Adventures area of the website (the url is listed below) in order to find specific titles appropriate for elementary students. The best way to really pick up and look through Marvel Adventures titles that could work in your classroom is to browse the kid's section of your local comic book shop or larger bookseller.

www.marvel.com/comics/Marvel_Adventures

DC COMICS

As the second member of the "top two," DC Comics is best known for its popular characters like Batman, Superman, and Wonder Woman. DC Comics offers child-appropriate versions of its comics under their Johnny DC imprint. On their website, you'll find comic books as well as softcover graphic novels and trade paperbacks of popular titles such as *Teen Titans Go!, Justice League Adventures, The Batman Strikes, Justice League Unlimited,* and *Superman Adventures,* as well as titles based on the Powerpuff Girls, Scooby-Doo, and various Warner Brothers and Cartoon Network characters.

www.dccomics.com/dckids

GEMSTONE PUBLISHING

Gemstone publishes the ever-popular Walt Disney Comics. These fictional comics are based on favorite classic Disney characters like Donald Duck, Mickey Mouse, and Uncle Scrooge.

www.gemstonepub.com/disney

DISNEY BOOKS

Disney also offers several graphica titles based on their popular Disney movies and TV shows like *Lilo and Stitch, The Lion King, Finding Nemo, Cars, Kid Gravity,* and *Gorilla, Gorilla.* When you visit the Disney Books website, scroll down and click on the "Comic Book/Graphic Novels" link on the left side of the screen to find out more.

http://disneybooks.disney.go.com/index.html

FIRST SECOND :01

First Second publishes creative, original titles in both fiction and nonfiction written for various age groups. Titles offered aren't separated by age or appropriateness, so you'll want to check them yourself.

http://www.firstsecondbooks.com/collection.html

DARK HORSE COMICS

If you have readers who obsess over *Star Wars,* Dark Horse publishes the kid friendly Star Wars: Clone Wars Adventures series in graphic novels and trade paperbacks. They're also reviving The Gremlins, a comic book series first introduced in a partnership between Disney Studios and children's book author Roald Dahl in 1943. Not all of Dark Horse's offerings are appropriate for younger readers, so use the following link to go directly to their kids' titles.

www.darkhorse.com/zones/kids/index.php

PUBLIC SQUARE BOOKS

A major publisher of graphica in Spanish, Public Square Books sells both original and translated titles. Many of their offerings are based on popular kids' shows from Fox and the Cartoon Network. They have a large selection, but not all of their titles are appropriate for younger children, and the site doesn't offer a way to differentiate between those that are and those that aren't.

www.publicsquarebooks.com

TOKYOPOP

With literally tons of books in print, Tokyopop covers a wide berth of titles and often can be found in some of the larger bookstores. Titles include child-friendly favorites such as *Pirates of the Caribbean, Avatar the Last Air Bender, Finding Nemo, Fairly Odd Parents, Bambi, Barbie, The Incredibles, Greatest Stars of the NBA, Mucha Lucha, SpongeBob SquarePants, Shrek, That's So Raven, Lizzie McGuire, Lilo and Stitch, Madagascar, Spy Kids, Totally Spies, Chicken Little, Power Rangers,* and *Transformers,* just to name a few! They also offer manga in the format of bridge comics—though only a handful of them. Tokyopop publishes manga for various audiences; when you visit their website, filter the selections by "A" (for all ages), which will take you to their more kid-friendly titles. If you register with the site, you can look at clips of their titles for free.

www.tokyopop.com/shop/browse

PAPERCUTZ

Becoming popular in their own right for their updated revival of The Hardy Boys and Nancy Drew series, Papercutz is a company on the fast track. They offer age-appropriate graphic novel series like Totally Spies, Zorro, and Tales from the Crypt. Word has it that they've also acquired and plan to update the quintessential educational comic series Classics Illustrated under a new banner called Classics Illustrated Deluxe. Look for them at larger bookstores, or go to their website for direct purchase.

www.papercutz.com

EDUCATIONAL PUBLISHERS

ROSEN CLASSROOM

Rosen offers graphic novels in varying ranges of interest and difficulty under its imprint Rosen Graphica. The imprint focuses on nonfiction and offers several titles that are appropriate for content area instruction, including biographies, history, mysteries, mythologies, disasters, civil war battles, black heroes, dinosaurs, discoveries, World War II battles, forensic science, and extreme careers. They sell their titles individually or in small-group instructional packs, and several of them are offered in dual levels of difficulty; as a result, your lower and higher readers can read graphica in the same content area!

www.rosenclassroom.com

ABDO PUBLISHING

Abdo distributes library-bound, durable versions of graphica from Marvel, Papercutz, and various other publishers through its sister companies Spotlight and Magic Wagon.

www.abdopublishing.com

SCHOLASTIC

Many teachers are unaware that Scholastic has its own graphica imprint called Graphix. Available through classroom book orders, book fairs, and local bookstores, Graphix publishes graphic novels based on popular series like the Baby-Sitters Club and Goosebumps, with the promise of more to come.

www.scholastic.com/graphix

CAPSTONE PUBLISHERS: STONE ARCH, CAPSTONE PRESS, AND RED BRICK LEARNING

This one's a little tricky, so bear with me. Stone Arch, Capstone Press, and Red Brick are all sister companies within the Capstone Publishers group of companies. All three offer graphica, and some of their titles overlap. This is because Capstone Press and Stone Arch distribute to libraries, whereas Red Brick distributes to curriculum areas (classroom teachers). So, if you want library-bound titles, go with Stone Arch and Capstone Press. If you want paperback titles and small-group instructional packs, stick with Red Brick.

STONE ARCH

Stone Arch (library company) sells graphic novels and bridge comics to libraries, and they have a huge selection. My readers really like their Graphic Sparks, Graphic Flash, and Graphic Revolve series, as well as characters like Jimmy Sniffles and Tiger Moth: Insect Ninja. You can find out more on their website by clicking on "Our Products" and then going to "Graphic Novels."

www.stonearchbooks.com

CAPSTONE PRESS

Capstone Press (library company) also sells to libraries and features its own Graphic Library collection. Many titles in this collection are available in both English and Spanish, and they focus on nonfiction areas such as history, social studies, biographies, disasters, and inventions. Capstone Press also offers a science series that features Max Axiom: Super Scientist, who explains science concepts using kid-friendly graphica.

www.capstonepress.com

RED BRICK

As mentioned before, Red Brick is the curriculum company sister to Stone Arch and Capstone Press, so the titles offered are the same. The difference is that Red Brick offers those titles in paperback and small-group instructional packs instead of single hardbacks. Thus, Red Brick has the nonfiction Graphic Library titles in English and Spanish that Capstone Press sells, as well as the fiction graphic novels and bridge comics from Stone Arch.

To find the softcover versions of Capstone Press's titles, go to Red Brick's website, click on "Our Products," and scroll down to "Graphic Library." To find the Stone Arch titles in softcover, do the same thing, but scroll down to "Kid's Choice" and search their "Fiction" section for collections with "graphic" in the title.

While you're there, check out Red Brick's interactive books. These are the graphica-based discs that you can play on your computer for fluency practice, which I mentioned in Chapter 9. They'd also make a great workstation. To see which Red Brick titles include discs, type "interactive book" (not books) into their website's search engine.

www.redbricklearning.com

GARETH STEVENS

The Gareth Stevens collection of graphica is based on history, legends, myths, and timeless tales. It also includes a selection of biographies, and several titles are available in Spanish. To find out more, go to their website and search for "graphic novel" (not novels), and off you go!

www.garethstevens.com

DK

DK, creator of the popular Eyewitness series, publishes a few historical fiction graphic novels. With titles like *The Terror Trail, The Curse of the Crocodile God,* and *Instruments of Death,* you'll definitely want to preview the collection to make sure the titles are appropriate for your students. For more information, go to their site and search for "graphic readers."

www.dk.com/schools

PHONICS COMICS

These short graphic novels are great for many struggling and transitional readers. They'll really enjoy them; the panels and artwork aren't too busy, which makes them easier to navigate. You can certainly feel the phonics-based bias at times, but overall, most of these titles don't come across as too contrived.

www.innovativekids.com

STECK-VAUGHN

Steck-Vaughn offers two types of graphica that will interest your students: their Timeline collection and their Lynx collection. The Timeline collection is a series of historical fiction based on major social studies topics. Each title has a biographical key so that readers can differentiate between fictional characters in the book and historical figures that really existed. The texts are intermittently sprinkled with factual articles, making this collection a great bridge comic option. The Timeline titles are available in small-group instructional packs and are appropriate for readers in upper elementary and middle school.

The Steck-Vaughn Lynx program links fiction graphica with nonfiction science and social studies texts (mentioned in Chapter 5), which makes for a terrific paired concept reading activity. These titles are available in small-group instructional packs and are appropriate for use with upper elementary readers as well as intermediate-level readers.

www.steckvaughn.com/timeline
www.steckvaughn.com/lynx

APPENDIX F

COMIC PANEL SKETCH TEMPLATES

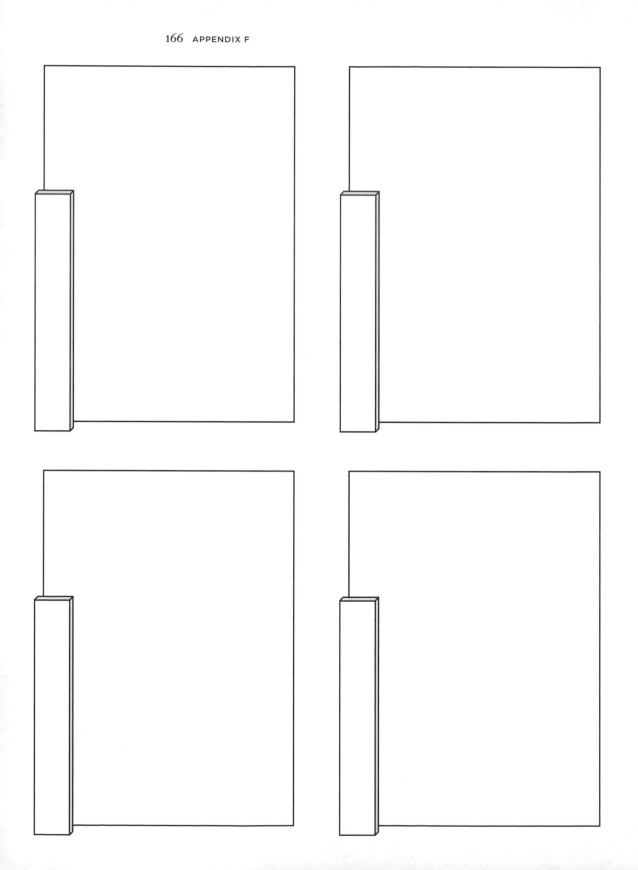

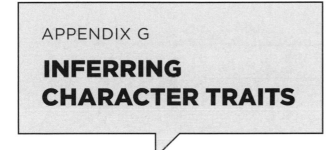

APPENDIX G

INFERRING CHARACTER TRAITS

CHARACTER STUDY

Student: _____

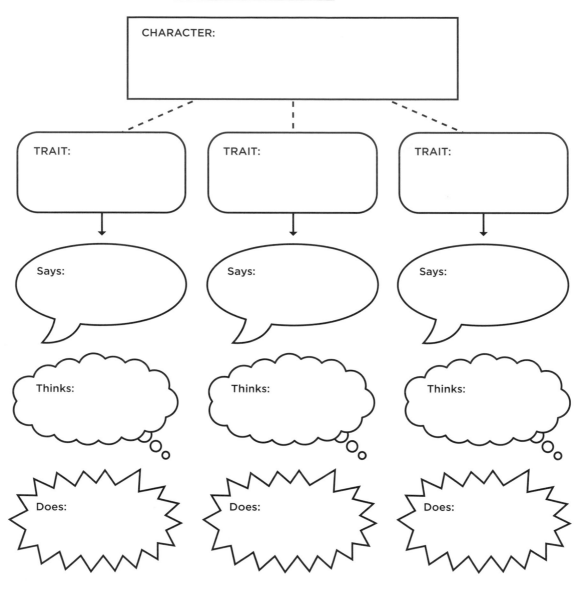

CHARACTER STUDY

Student: _____   Character: _____

SAID	THOUGHT	DID

CHARACTER STUDY

Student: _____

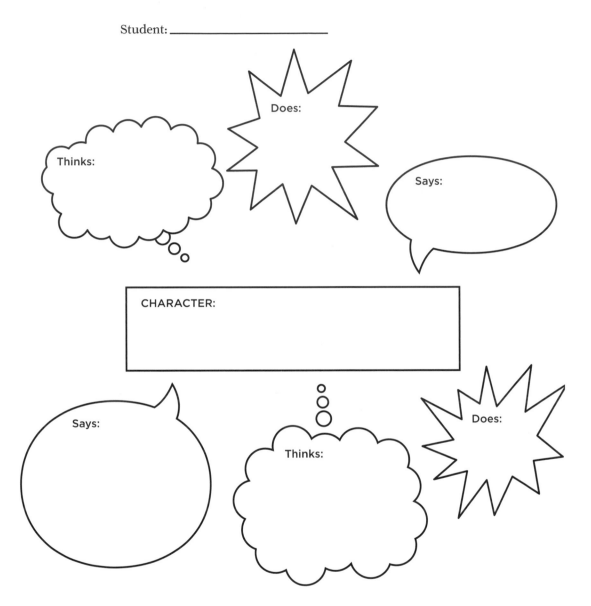

FACIAL EXPRESSIONS CHART

Copyright Learning and Teaching Scotland

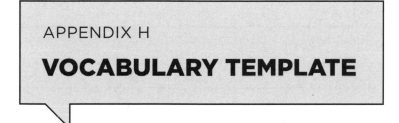

APPENDIX H

VOCABULARY TEMPLATE

New Word	Clues from the DIALOGUE	Clues from the ILLUSTRATIONS	Clues from the TEXT	What I INFER it means

Dictionary Meaning:

New Word	Clues from the DIALOGUE	Clues from the ILLUSTRATIONS	Clues from the TEXT	What I INFER it means

Dictionary Meaning:

New Word	Clues from the DIALOGUE	Clues from the ILLUSTRATIONS	Clues from the TEXT	What I INFER it means

Dictionary Meaning:

New Word	Clues from the DIALOGUE	Clues from the ILLUSTRATIONS	Clues from the TEXT	What I INFER it means

Dictionary Meaning:

APPENDIX I

SPEECH BUBBLE EXAMPLES

REFERENCES

Allen, Janet. 1999. *Words, Words, Words: Teaching Vocabulary in Grades 4-12*. Portland, ME: Stenhouse.

Allington, Richard A. 2005. *What Really Matters for Struggling Readers: Designing Research-Based Programs*. 2nd ed. Boston: Allyn and Bacon.

Association for Library Service to Children Research and Development Committee. 2006. "Graphic Novels for Children: Should They Be Considered Literature?" *Children and Libraries: Journal of the Association for Library Service to Children* 4 (3): 49-51.

Atwell, Nancie. 2007. *The Reading Zone: How to Help Kids Become Skilled, Passionate, Habitual, Critical Readers*. New York: Scholastic.

Behler, Anne. 2006. "Getting Started with Graphic Novels: A Guide for the Beginner." *Reference & User Services Quarterly* 46 (2): 16-21.

Brand, Max, and Gayle Brand. 2006. *Practical Fluency: Classroom Perspectives, Grades K-6*. Portland, ME: Stenhouse.

Brenner, Robin. 2006. "Graphic Novels 101: FAQ." *The Horn Book Magazine* 82 (2): 125.

Carrick, Lila Ubert. 2006. "Reader's Theater Across the Curriculum." In *Fluency Instruction: Research-Based Practices*, ed. Timothy Rasinski, Camille Blachowicz, and Kristin Lems. New York: Guilford.

Cart, Michael. 2005. "A Graphic Novel Explosion." *Booklist* 101 (14): 1301.

———. 2006. "My Love Affair with the Comics." *Booklist* 102 (14): 44.

Cary, Stephen. 2004. *Going Graphic: Comics at Work in the Multilingual Classroom*. Portsmouth. NH: Heinemann.

Crawford, Philip. 2004. "A Novel Approach: Using Graphic Novels to Attract Reluctant Readers." *Library Media Connection* 22 (5): 26-28.

Cunningham, Annie E., and Keith E. Stanovich. 2001. "What Reading Does for the Mind." *American Educator* 22 (1/2): 8–15.

Cunningham, Patricia M., and Richard L. Allington. 1994. *Classrooms That Work: They Can All Read and Write*. 4th ed. New York: HarperCollins College.

Cunningham, Andie, and Ruth Shagoury. 2005. *Starting with Comprehension: Reading Strategies for the Youngest Learners*. Portland, ME: Stenhouse.

Curriculum Review. 2005. "Serious ESL Lessons Await Students in the Funny Pages." *Curriculum Review* 45 (2): 10.

Davis, Randall. 1997. "Comics: A Multi-Dimensional Teaching Aid in Integrated-Skills Classes." *Studies in Social Sciences and Humanities*. Nagoya, Japan: Nagoya City University. Also available online at http://www.esl-lab.com/research/comics.htm.

Eisner, Will. 1985. *Comics and Sequential Art*. Tamarac, FL: Poorhouse.

Ezarik, Melissa. 2003. "Comics in the Classroom." *District Administration* 39 (4): 42.

Fallis, Chris. 2005. "Graphic Generation." Young Adult Library Services 3 (4): 16.

Fine, Jana. 2005. "Ouch! An Interview with Papercutz Publisher Terry Nantier." *Young Adult Library Services* 3 (4): 12-13.

Foster, Katy. 2004. "Graphic Novels in Libraries: An Expert's Opinion." *Library Media Connection* 22 (5): 30.

Fountas, Irene C., and Gay Su Pinnell. 2001. *Guiding Readers and Writers, Grades 3-6: Teaching Comprehension, Genre, and Content Literacy*. Portsmouth, NH: Heinemann.

Freeman, Matt. 1997. "The Case for Comics." *Reading Today* 15 (3): 3.

George, Stephen. 2003. "Comics with Class." *Better Homes and Gardens*, June.

Gorman, Michele. 2003. *Getting Graphic! Using Graphic Novels to Promote Literacy with Preteens and Teens*. Worthington, OH: Linworth.

Guevara, Michael. 2006. "Girls Outdistance, Outscore Boys in Literacy." *Texas Voices: Texas Council of Teachers of English Language Arts* 20 (1): 9.

Harvey, Stephanie, and Anne Goudvis. 2007. *Strategies That Work: Teaching Comprehension for Understanding and Engagement*. 2nd ed. Portland, ME: Stenhouse.

Keene, Ellin Oliver, and Susan Zimmermann. 2007. *Mosaic of Thought: The Power of Comprehension Strategy Instruction*. 2nd ed. Portsmouth, NH: Heinemann.

Kerr, Sherry, and T. H. Culhane. *The Humble Comic: Possibilities for Developing Literacy Skills and Learning Content*. Pearson Learning. http://www.pearsonlearning.com/correlation/rsp/ResearchPaper_Comic.pdf. Accessed Sept. 2006.

Krashen, Stephen. 2004. *The Power of Reading: Insights from the Research*. 2nd ed. Portsmouth, NH: Heinemann.

Lavin, Michael. 1998. "Comic Books and Graphic Novels for Libraries: What to Buy." *Serials Review* 24 (2): 31.

Lyga, Allyson A. W., and Barry Lyga. 2004. *Graphic Novels in Your Media Center: A Definitive Guide.* Westport, CT: Libraries Unlimited.

McCloud, Scott. 1993. *Understanding Comics: The Invisible Art.* New York: HarperPerennial.

McGrath, Charles. 2004. "Not Funnies." *New York Times,* July 11.

McPherson, Keith. 2006. "Graphic Literacy." *Teacher Librarian* 31 (4): 30-32.

Mendez, Teresa. 2004. "Hamlet Too Hard? Try a Comic Book." *Christian Science Monitor,* October 12.

Miller, Debbie. 2002. *Reading with Meaning: Teaching Comprehension in the Primary Grades.* Portland, ME: Stenhouse.

Raiteri, Steve. 2006. "Graphic Novels." *Library Journal* 131 (1): 86.

Rasinski, Timothy V. 2003. *The Fluent Reader: Oral Reading Strategies for Building Word Recognition, Fluency, and Comprehension.* New York: Scholastic.

Rasinski, Timothy, Camille Blachowicz, and Kristen Lems. 2006. *Fluency Instruction: Research-Based Best Practices.* New York: Guilford.

Reid, Calvin. 2005. "US Graphic Novel Market Hits $200M." *Publishers Weekly* 252 (16): 15.

Routman, Regie. 2003. *Reading Essentials: The Specifics You Need to Teach Reading Well.* Portsmouth, NH: Heinemann.

Samuels, S. Jay, and Alan E. Farstrup. 2006. *What Research Has to Say About Fluency Instruction.* Newark, DE: International Reading Association.

Schwarz, Gretchen. 2006. "Expanding Literacies Through Graphic Novels." *English Journal* 95 (6): 58-96.

Simpson, Carol Mann. 2005. *Copyright For Schools: A Practical Guide*. 4th ed. Worthington, OH: Linworth.

Snowball, Clare. 2005. "Teenage Reluctant Readers and Graphic Novels." *Young Adult Library Services* 3 (4): 43-45.

Szymusiak, Karen, and Franki Sibberson. 2001. *Beyond Leveled Books: Supporting Transitional Readers in Grades 2–5*. Portland, ME: Stenhouse.

Ujiie, Joanne, and Stephen Krashen. 1996. "Comic Book Reading, Reading Enjoyment, and Pleasure Reading Among Middle Class and Chapter I Middle School Students." *Reading Improvement* 33 (1): 51-54.

Versaci, Rocco. 2001. "How Comics Can Change the Way Our Students See Literature: One Teacher's Perspective." *English Journal* 91 (2): 61-67.

Wertham, Frederic. 1954. *Seduction of the Innocent*. New York: Rinehart.

White, Bailey. 1993. *Mama Makes Up Her Mind and Other Dangers of Southern Living*. New York: Vintage.

Wilhelm, Jeffery D. 2004. *Reading Is Seeing: Learning to Visualize Scenes, Characters, Ideas, and Text Worlds to Improve Comprehension and Reflective Reading*. New York: Scholastic.

Williams, Neil. 1995. "The Comic Book as Course Book: Why and How." Paper presented at the Annual Meeting of the Teachers of English to Speakers of Other Languages, Long Beach, CA, March 26–April 1.

Yang, Gene. 2003. "Comics in Education." Humble Comics. http://www.geneyang.com/comicsedu.

INDEX

Page numbers followed by an *f* indicate figures.